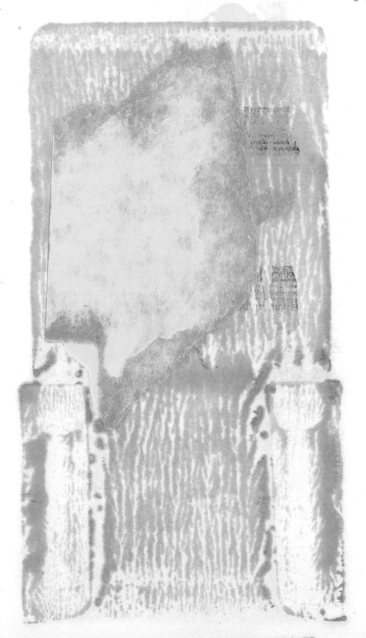

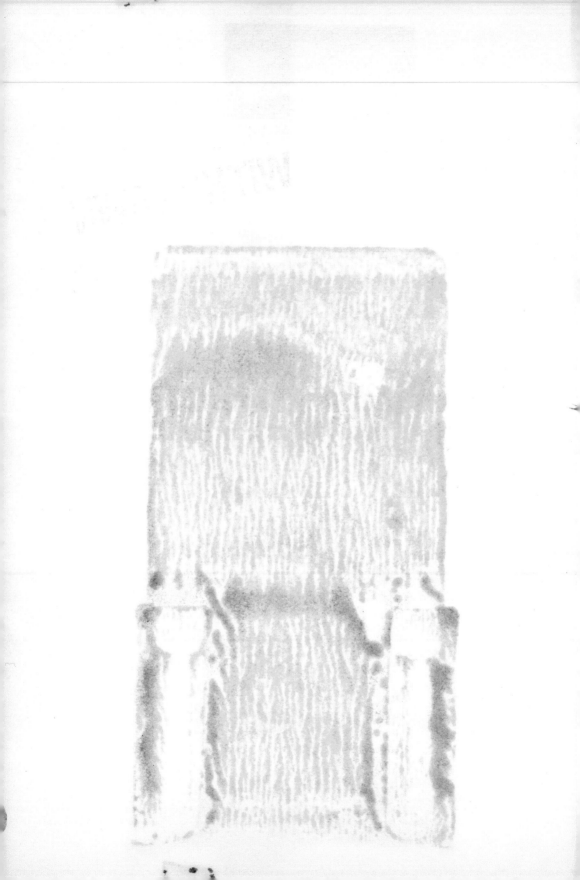

RICHMOND

IN TIME OF WAR

HOUGHTON MIFFLIN RESEARCH SERIES

Number 5

HOUGHTON MIFFLIN RESEARCH SERIES

RICHMOND

IN TIME

OF WAR

Edited by

William J. Kimball

MARY BALDWIN COLLEGE

HOUGHTON MIFFLIN COMPANY · BOSTON

The Riverside Press Cambridge

The selections reprinted in this collection are used by permission of and special arrangement with the proprietors of their respective copyrights.

From *The Beleaguered City* by Alfred Hoyt Bill, by permission of Afred A. Knopf, Inc.

From *A Diary from Dixie* by Mary Boykin Chesnut, by permission of Houghton Mifflin Company.

"The Confederate Tradition of Richmond" by Douglas Southall Freeman; reprinted by permission of Mrs. Freeman.

From the article "When War Came to Richmond" by Douglas Southall Freeman, by permission of *The Richmond News Leader*.

From *R. E. Lee* by Douglas Southall Freeman. Used by permission of Charles Scribner's Sons.

From *Recollections, Grave and Gay* by Constance Cary Harrison, copyright 1911 Charles Scribner's Sons; renewal copyright 1939 Fairfax Harrison. Used by permission of Charles Scribner's Sons.

From *Civil War Prisons* by William Best Hesseltine; published by The Ohio State University Press; selection reprinted with the author's permission.

From *A Rebel War Clerk's Diary* by John B. Jones, by permission of the Old Hickory Bookshop, New York.

From *Pickett and His Men* by Mrs. G. E. Pickett, by permission of J. B. Lippincott Company.

From *Reminiscences of Peace and War* by Mrs. Roger A. Pryor, copyright 1904 by The Macmillan Company, and used with their permission.

From *Richmond, Its People and Its Story* by Mary Newton Stanard, by permission of J. B. Lippincott Company.

From *Hidden Things Brought to Light* by Ernest Taylor Walthall, by permission of The Dietz Press, Inc.

From *St. Paul's Church, Its Historic Years and Memorials* by Elizabeth Wright Weddell; published by The William Byrd Press; selections reprinted by permission of the Woman's Auxiliary of St. Paul's Church, Richmond.

Cover photograph: Courtesy of Library of Congress (Photo by Brady)

CONTENTS

DOCUMENTARY SOURCES

Jefferson Davis
Robert E. Lee
Heros von Borcke
Mary Boykin Chesnut
Virginia Tunstall Clay
Varina Howell Davis
T. C. DeLeon
George Cary Eggleston
Dr. J. R. Gildersleeve
Constance Cary Harrison
John B. Jones
Judith W. McGuire
Rev. Charles Minnigerode
Mrs. G. E. Pickett
Mrs. Roger A. Pryor
Sallie A. Brock Putnam
William Howard Russell
Mrs. D. Giraud Wright
and other contemporaries

Alfred Hoyt Bill
Douglas Southall Freeman
William Best Hesseltine
and other historians

The Richmond *Enquirer, Examiner, Whig,* etc.
Official Records of the Union and Confederate Armies
Messages and Papers of the Confederacy

PUBLISHER'S NOTE

The use of selected research materials no longer needs justification — if indeed it ever did. That they ease the strain on overtaxed libraries and aid the instructor in teaching the heart of the research method by giving him control of material which all his class is using, there is no dispute. But there are other advantages worth noting.

A genuine grasp of research method is of lifelong value. The habit of sifting evidence, weighing bias, winnowing fact from opinion, assessing the judgments of others, and reaching an opinion of one's own with due regard for the possibility that new-found evidence may change it tomorrow — this is far more than a means to better grades and better papers; it is a way of mature and responsible thinking which can affect one's competence in every aspect of living. It is the aim of this book, and of the others in the Houghton Mifflin Research Series, to help the student take a stride in this direction.

The aim has been to pack into these pages enough central documentary material to give useful practice in choosing a limited topic within a broader area, scanning a large body of material, and hence in learning to reject that which is not immediately relevant and to select that which is. The major emphasis is thus placed, as it should be, on the selection, evaluation, organization, and synthesis of materials. The mechanics of note-taking, outlining, and footnote and bibliographical form are treated in every handbook and rhetoric, and are not discussed here. For accurate documentation, however, the page numbers of original sources are given in heavy type immediately *after* the material from the page.

Within the limits of these broad aims the book can be used in many ways: (a) for short practice papers stressing the mechanics of research technique; (b) for full-length research papers using only materials here provided; and (c) as a springboard for papers which involve use of the library and additional reading, either historical or literary. Literature as such has been rigidly excluded, partly for reasons of length and of general student interest, and partly because only the gifted or the specially trained student can at this stage competently handle the very different problems of research and of criticism at the same time. For such students there is ample opportunity to step from the present materials into the relevant literature of special interest to him.

The author has appended lists of suggested topics for short and long papers and for library research, to give both practice and example to encourage the kinds of reading and thinking essential to competent research in any field.

PREFACE

Whether or not it was militarily proper to move the capital of the Confederacy to Richmond in May, 1861, has often been the subject of debate when Civil War buffs have gathered. But there were reasons in 1861 for moving the capital to Richmond, and it was done. Almost overnight this quiet city on picturesque hills by the "falls of the James" became the heart of the Confederacy and a seat of war. The population of approximately 38,000 more than doubled before 1865 and the city that had been the capital of the commonwealth since 1779 was never to return to its romantic past. It became the most "interesting" city of the Confederacy, and its history during the war holds for many a fascinating charm.

The purpose, then, of this presentation of Richmond in time of war as a subject for research is twofold. It is hoped, first, that the student will learn to appreciate and evaluate primary and secondary source materials; and second, that in doing so he will succumb to the charm of the city. In short, why should he not enjoy the subject about which he is writing?

Collected in these pages are over two hundred documents, each one keyed directly or indirectly to life in Richmond during the Civil War. Many are primary sources not available to the student through the facilities of the average college library. Therefore, without prohibitive costs and extensive traveling, he has here before him "pictures" of practically every facet of life in this struggling city during its most trying days. He can, with these materials, reconstruct the unflinching patriotism and the dissembling cowardice; the lush life of some and the near-starvation existence of others; the gay society and the heart-rending gloom; the hope and the fear; the suffering and the whole. In no sense, of course, do these documents even begin to exhaust the material relevant to the capital of the Confederacy during this time. But enough is given to enable the student to put his finger on the pulse of the Confederacy and feel its health rise and fall until eventual death.

Because it is felt that organization and arrangement are integral parts of the entire research process, there has been no attempt to organize the materials in this book other than to place them in a rough chronological order as indicated by the five parts of the text. Documents which cover an extended period of time are inserted where they seem most relevant. The student is cautioned to note that in some instances there are conflicting descriptions or explanations of the same incident; and this is good, for he must arrive at what is either the view of the majority or his own interpretation grounded upon the fact that it is possible to approach certainty only after sifting and re-sifting the evidence.

Where it has seemed necessary or advisable, brief explanatory material has been provided. Omissions in the text are indicated by ellipses or editorial explanations. Whenever possible, original spellings and constructions have been retained, and the use of the Latin *sic* has been reserved for those places where unconventional spelling or syntax might confuse the student.

Before reading the text, the student is urged to look over the lists of topics and questions at the end of the book for aid in choosing his own topic. The suggested topics for library research, which appear in these lists, give him an opportunity to become familiar with his library and its discipline. These aids are all directed, however, to the primary function of this text — to give the student an opportunity to evaluate and interpret, for this is the heart of the library research project.

I am indebted to the members of the Virginia State Library in Richmond, the personnel of the Confederate Museum in Richmond, Miss Helena C. Koiner of the Alderman Library at the University of Virginia, and especially to Mr. Henry F. Thoma and his staff at Houghton Mifflin for invaluable suggestions and assistance in compiling the material for this book. It is impossible to thank personally everyone who has warmly and willingly listened to me and talked with me about this subject.

WILLIAM J. KIMBALL

Staunton, Virginia

1861

"On to Richmond"

1861

No. 1 Douglas Southall Freeman, *R. E. Lee,* New York, Charles Scribner's Sons, 1934-35, vol. I (4 vols.).

Richmond had been a quiet city of 37,000 people when madness had seized the country, a place of peace and pleasantness. John Smith had come there at Whitsuntide in the year when Jamestown had been settled; a fort had been erected at the "falls of the James" before the massacre of 1622; slowly through the eighteenth century it had been built up until, in 1779, it had become the capital of the commonwealth, in succession to Williamsburg. On picturesque hills, that followed a wide bend in the river, successful merchants had reared ample homes. Flour that was sent "across the line" to South America had early been stenciled with the city's name; a capitol that Jefferson himself had modeled after an old Roman temple at Nimes had been erected on the finest eminence. A generation later a canal had been started that was to link Richmond with the headwaters of the Ohio and rescue for Virginia the trade of the old Northwest that New York was diverting through the Erie. John Marshall had lived in Richmond and had been buried there; Edgar Allan Poe had called it home. To its large hotels the wealthy planters had come; from its platforms Clay, Webster, Thackeray, and Dickens had spoken. Wealthy for the time, with strong banks, varied manufactories, profitable shipping, and ample railroad connections with almost every part of the state, boasting a state arsenal and a large rolling mill, Richmond was the heart of Virginia, financially and economically. Most of all she was rich in her people. None of them had a mighty fortune; few of them were very poor, but nearly all of them had lived long in the town and had the homogeneity not less of under- **page 460/** standing than of blood. Together they rejoiced; as one they labored. *Noblesse oblige* was written larger in the civic code than any ordinance the common hall ever drafted. As Whigs and as Democrats, as "Union men" and secessionists, the voters had divided often and violently; but always for their city's honor they had been a unit. Fire and pestilence and the gray adversity that had followed "flush times" had left them like-minded. Save for the long-forgotten Indian fights and a brush with the British, when Arnold had occupied the place in 1781, Richmond had never heard the clash of combat, but now that the evil day was come she had cast her lot wholeheartedly with the South. All that she had symbolized in peace was to be forgotten in the battles that were to be waged for her. Alarms were to bewilder her; the first laughter was to stun her; but soon she was to show the staunchness of her soul. **page 461/**

No. 2 Daily Richmond Examiner, April 15, 1861, p. 2.

The news of the capture of Fort Sumter was greeted with unbounded enthusiasm in this city. Everybody we met seemed to be perfectly happy. Indeed, until
this occasion we did not know how happy men could be. Everybody abuses war,
and yet it has ever been the favourite and most honored pursuit of men; and the
women and children admire and love war ten times as much as the men. The boys
pulled down the stars and stripes from the top of the Capitol, (some of the boys
were sixty years old) and very properly run [sic] up the flag of the Southern Confederacy in its place. What the women did we don't precisely know, but learned
from rumour that they praised South Carolina to the skies, abused Virginia, put it
to the Submissionists hot and heavy with their two-edged swords, and wound up the
evening's ceremonies by playing and singing secession songs until fifteen minutes
after twelve on Saturday night. — The boys exploded an infinite number of crackers;
the price of tar has risen twenty-five percent, and sky-rockets and Roman candles
can be had at no price, the whole stock in trade having been used up Saturday
night. We had great firing of cannon, all sorts of processions, an infinite number of
grandiloquent, hifaluting speeches, and some drinking of healths, which has not
improved healths; for one half the people we have met since are hoarse from long
and loud talking, and the other half have a slight headache, it may be, from long
and patriotic libations.

No. 3 Daily Richmond Examiner, April 23, 1861, p. 3.

Distinguished Arrivals

The Honorable Alexander H. Stephens, Vice President of the Confederate
States, reached this city yesterday morning, by the Southern train, and took up
quarters at the Exchange.

General Lee, late of the United States Army, arrived from Alexandria by the
Northern train in the afternoon, and is stopping at the Spotswood Hotel. Both
gentlemen have business of importance with the Governor.

*No. 4 John B. Jones, A Rebel War Clerk's Diary, New York, Old Hickory Book-
shop, 1935, vol. I (2 vols.).*

April 27, 1861: We have had a terrible alarm. The tocsin was sounded in the
public square, and thousands have been running hither and thither to know its
meaning. Dispatches have been posted about the city, purporting to have been

received by the governor, with the startling information that the U. S. war steamer Pawnee is coming up the James River for the purpose of shelling the city.

All the soldiery, numbering some thousands, are marching down to Rocketts, and forming in line of battle on the heights commanding the approaches. The howitzers are there, frowning defiance; and two long French bronze guns are slowly passing through Main Street in the same direction. One of them has just broken down, and lies abandoned in front of the Post-Office. Even civilians, by hundreds, are hurrying with shot-guns and pistols to the scene of action, and field officers are galloping through the streets. Although much apprehension is apparent on many faces, it is but just to say that the population generally are resolved to make a determined defense. . . .

It was a false alarm, if not something worse. I fear it is an invention of the enemy to divert us from the generally conceived policy of attacking Washington, and rousing up Maryland in the rear of Lincoln. page 28/

No. 5 *Official Records of the Union and Confederate Armies,* series 1, volume LI, part II, Washington, Government Printing Office, 1897.

Richmond, May 7, 1861.
(Received 5 O'clock 8th.)

L. P. Walker:

I believe there is treachery here. Intelligent and distinguished men believe Virginia on the very brink of being carried back, and say no man but President Davis can save her. The people will rally around him; they universally call for his presence. There is disappointment that he does not assume entire directions of affairs here. Louisiana troops reported to Cabell, Cabell sent them to Bonham, Bonham to Lee. Lee orders them to Harper's Ferry. Great dissatisfaction prevails here. South Carolina troops refuse to move unless under orders from Montgomery. Military control of Virginia is essential to the interests of the Confederate States. I doubt if there are 5,000 Virginians armed and equipped. Letcher has ordered volunteers to remain at home on plea of want of arms, while there are abundance of arms in the State in the opinion of persons capable of judging. page 71/

D. G. Duncan

No. 6 William Howard Russell, *My Diary North and South,* London, Bradbury and Evans, 1863, vol. I (2 vols.).

> [*Sir William Russell was an English war correspondent who was in this country from approximately March, 1861, until April, 1862. While here, he traveled rather extensively, and although he was not in Richmond, some of his observations of the men who were soon to take up residence there are interesting.*]

May 9, 1861: I had an opportunity of observing the President very closely: he did not impress me as favourably as I had expected, though he is certainly a very different looking man from Mr. Lincoln. He is like a gentleman — has a slight, light figure, little exceeding middle height, and holds himself erect and straight. He was dressed in a rustic suit of slate-coloured stuff, with a black silk handkerchief round his neck; his manner is plain, and rather reserved and drastic; his head is well formed, with a fine full forehead, square **page 249/** and high, covered with innumerable fine lines and wrinkles, features regular, though the cheek-bones are too high, and the jaws too hollow to be handsome; the lips are thin, flexible, and curved, the chin square, well defined; the nose very regular, with wide nostrils; and the eyes deep set, large and full — one seems nearly blind, and is partly covered with a film, owing to excruciating attacks of neuralgia and tic. Wonderful to relate, he does not chew, and is neat and clean-looking, with hair trimmed, and boots brushed. The expression of his face is anxious, he has a very haggard, care-worn, and pain-drawn look, though no trace of anything but the utmost confidence and the greatest decision could be detected in his conversation. . . .

I mentioned that I had seen great military preparations through the South, and was astonished at the alacrity with which the people sprang to arms. "Yes, sir," he remarked, and his tone of voice and manner of speech are rather remarkable for what are considered Yankee peculiarities, "In Eu-rope" (Mr. Seward also indulges in that pronunciation) "they laugh at us because of our fondness for military titles and displays. All your travellers in this country have commented on the number of generals, and colonels, and majors all over the States. But the fact is, we are a military people, and these signs of the fact were ignored. We are not less military because we have no great standing armies. But perhaps we are the only people in the world where gentlemen go to a military academy who do not intend to follow the profession of arms." **page 250/**

No. 7   William Howard Russell, *My Diary North and South*, London, Bradbury and Evans, 1863, vol. 1 (2 vols.).

> *[There is some peculiarity in the diarist's chronology, for this entry is dated May 8, and the one following it is dated May 9. As we have seen, an entry some nine pages earlier in the book was also dated May 9.]*

May 8, 1861: Early this morning, as usual, my faithful Wigfall [Senator Louis T. of Texas] comes in and sits by my bedside, and passing his hands through his locks, pours out his ideas with wonderful lucidity and odd affectation of logic all his own. "We are a peculiar people, sir! You don't understand us, and you can't understand us, because we are known to you only by Northern writers and Northern papers, who know nothing of us themselves, or misrepresent what they do know. We are an agricultural people; we are a primitive but a civilized people. We have no cities — we don't want them. We have no literature — we don't need any yet. We have no press — we are glad of it. We do not require a press, because we go out and discuss all public questions from the stump with our people. We have no commercial marine — no navy — we don't want them. Your ships carry our produce, and you can protect your own vessels. We want no   page 258/   manufactures: we desire no trading, no mechanical or manufacturing classes. As long as we have our rice, our sugar, our tobacco, and our cotton, we can command wealth to produce all we want from those nations with which we are in amity, and to lay up money besides. But with the Yankees we will never trade — never. Not one pound of cotton shall ever go from the South to their accursed cities; not one ounce of their steel or their manufacturers shall ever cross our border." And so on. What the Senator who is preparing a bill for drafting the people into the army fears is, that the North will begin active operations before the South is ready for resistance. "Give us till November to drill our men, and we shall be irresistible." He deprecates any offensive movement, and is opposed to an attack on Washington, which many journals here advocate. page 259/

No. 8 *Official Records of the Union and Confederate Armies,* series 1, volume LI, Part II, Washington, Government Printing Office, 1897.

Richmond Va., May 11, 1861.

His Excellency Jefferson Davis:

Dear Sir: As you value our great cause hasten on to Richmond. Lincoln and Scott are, if I mistake not, covering by other demonstration a great movement upon Richmond. Suppose they should send suddenly up the York River, as they can, an army of 30,000 or more, there are no means at hand to repel them, and [if] their policy shown in Maryland gets footing here it will be a severe if not a fatal blow. Hasten, I pray you, to avert it. The very fact of your presence will almost answer. Hasten then, I entreat you, don't lose a day.   page 81/

Your old friend,

W. N. Pendleton

No. 9 Richmond *Daily Whig,* May 18, 1861, p. 3.

Subsistence

Though the market is nearly bare of Western hog meat, we are glad to learn that the stock of Virginia bacon — as good as the best — is quite ample. . . . Corn is also abundant, and prices have declined. Meal should come down also. With plenty of sweet middling and corn dodgers, we may laugh at our enemies who think they can starve us into terms. But from present appearances, subsistence will be cheaper in Richmond, during the summer months, than it has been for many years, within the same period.

No. 10   Mary Boykin Chesnut, *A Diary from Dixie,* Boston, Houghton Mifflin Company, 1949.

May 20, 1861: Lunched at Mrs. Davis's. Everything nice to eat, and I was ravenous. And she was as nice as the luncheon. When she is in the mood, I do not know so pleasant a person. She is awfully clever, always. We talked of this move from Montgomery to Richmond. Mr. Chesnut opposes it violently because this [Montgomery] is so central a position for our government. Then he wants our troops sent into Maryland to make our fight on the border, and to encompass Washington. I think these uncomfortable hotels will move the Congress. Our statesmen love their ease. And it will be so hot here in the summer. "I do hope they will go," Mrs. Davis said. "The Yankees will make it hot for us, go where we will; and if war comes . . ." "It has come," said I. "Yes, I fancy these dainty folks may even live to regret the fare of the Montgomery hotels." "Never."   **page 51/**

No. 11   Richmond *Daily Whig,* May 22, 1861, p. 3.

The Fair Grounds

Crowds of ladies and gentlemen repair every afternoon to the "Camp of Instruction" of the Virginia Volunteers, at the Hermitage Fair Grounds; to the encampment of the South Carolina Regiments, near the Reservoir, and to the other places of military interest, near the city, to view the battalion drills and dress parades. The proficiency of the Lexington Cadets, who are quartered at the first mentioned place, is something wonderful to behold, and worth going a long distance to see.

No. 12   Mary Newton Stanard, *Richmond, Its People and Its Story,* Philadelphia, J. P. Lippincott Company, 1923.

On that same historic April day, [April 12] the Convention sent William Ballard Preston, Alexander H. H. Stuart and George Randolph to Washington, to ask the President what his attitude toward the seceding states would be. He replied (quoting his inaugural address): "The power confided in me will be used to hold, occupy and possess the property and places belonging to the government, and to collect the duties and imports; but beyond what is necessary for these objects, there will be no invasion, no using of force against or among the people anywhere." Before the Commissioners could present this answer to the Convention, eagerly awaiting it in

Richmond, President Lincoln had called for 75,000 troops to reduce the seceding states, and asked Virginia for her quota. Governor Letcher declined to send a man from Virginia to make war on her sister states of the South. For once, party differences were forgotten in Richmond. People of every shade of opinion were bound together in a brotherhood to protect the rights of Southern States and defend Southern homes against an invading army. Virginia recognized in the President's call for troops a declaration of war. The peacefulness and quiet of Richmond had now become a tradition. Fierce agitation replaced the old tranquility and in the streets, the hotels, the drawing-rooms, nothing was heard but hot discussion. Men's pulses were feverish. Neighbors of opposite sides scowled fiercely at each other.   **page 163/** Young ladies wore Southern colors and would turn their backs on an admirer who was not for secession.

The cockade of South Carolina was everywhere worn. Everything, even the social life of young folk, centered around the Capitol where the Convention was in session. It was the habit of the young ladies to promenade with their gallants in the Capitol Square, in the evening, and enjoy the strains of a fine band stationed in the rostrum opposite City Hall and overlooking the Square.

The seriousness of the situation was reflected in the countenances and bearing of the Convention and in the grave debate which showed that many members who had been most earnest advocates of preserving the Union so long as it could be preserved with peace, were heart and soul with the South now that war was unavoidable. The spectators who had packed the hall were turned out and the Convention went into secret session, but instead of going home the people swarmed in the Square, waiting with intense anxiety to hear the fate of Virginia which they knew hung on the words that were being spoken within that building of many happenings, where the most solemn scene in Richmond's Drama was being enacted. On April 17th, the final vote was taken and Ordnance of Secession passed by 103 to 43 votes. The announcement made on the next morning was received with wildest joy by the people. The flag of the newly formed Southern Confederacy was run up on the staff on the roof of the Capitol. The crowd in the Square saluted it with cheers. The Custom House was taken in charge by military officers of the state and preparations to provide barracks for soldiers and commissary stores for their support began.   **page 164/**

No. 13   The Richmond *News Leader,* Bicentennial Issue, September 8, 1937.

When War Came to Richmond

DOUGLAS SOUTHALL FREEMAN

. . . about 8 o'clock on the morning of May 29 [1861] the waiting thousands on the north side of the James saw the Petersburg train come puffing importantly around the curve in Manchester. A few minutes later, a battery of artillery began to fire the Presidential salute; when the tall figure of the President emerged from the car, a roar went up. He manifestly was much fatigued, but he was smiling in his dignity and graceful in every movement — so thin that he seemed emaciated, yet in appearance younger than Richmond had expected to find him. **page 62/**

Unlike the military men, he was close-shaven, with his dark hair parted far on his left side and swirled over his high forehead in a half curl over the right temple. The lines of his mouth were thin and clean cut, determined but not severe. His granite-gray eyes shone with so bright a light that even those Richmonders who were closest to him never would have observed that his left eye was blind.

Carriages were waiting for the President and for his honorary escort of public officials and local celebrities that had gone over   **page 63/**   to Petersburg to receive him. The streets along the short ride to the Spotswood [Hotel] were jammed: The welcoming cheers were continuous; spring flowers were thrown in the way. When one girl missed her aim and saw her bouquet fall short of the carriage, Mr. Davis stopped the vehicle and had a servant pick up the posies, which he presented to Mrs. Wigfall, who rode with him. Then he drove on to the hotel entrance where half of Richmond seemed to be gathered. So insistent was the multitude that Mr. Davis, weary though he was, had to speak from his hotel window. **page 64/**

.   .   .   .

[After First Manassas] Richmond reflected and perhaps focused the fatal over-confidence of the Confederate people. . . .

The late summer and autumn of 1861 brought disease and death to Richmond boys . . . and misgivings, then fear and then panic seized the weak hearted. Talk was openly heard of abandoning Richmond, which nine months before, even the timid had affirmed the Federals could not capture. Then came momentary rejoicing in the feat of the ironclad Virginia-Merrimac, but this was followed by deeper depression.

The great popularity of Davis waned and then gave place to sharp and bitter criticism. Beauregard had been sent West; Johnston's friends in Richmond said that he was hampered at every turn by the President and by Secretary Benjamin, who had succeeded Pope Walker in the War Department. A few knew that "Stonewall" Jackson had tendered his resignation because of the Secretary's repeated interference with his command and had recalled it only at the instance of Governor Letcher.

When the first anniversary of the secession of Virginia came on April 17, 1862, the old exuberance and the vaunted confidence was gone. Shiloh had been fought just ten days before. Albert Sidney Johnston, regarded by many as the foremost of all the soldiers of the South, had been killed there. Some were whispering that New Orleans was doomed.

The chief content that Richmond had in the midst of all these disasters was the sight of troops from Manassas who marched through Richmond on their way to Yorktown on the very date that had seen, in 1861, the old flag come down from the capitol. The soldiers numbered about 8,000 and were under General James Long-street.

.   .   .   .

Richmond took heart from them. The city smiled, even when the boys took daffodils from outstretched hands and put them in their caps or into the barrels of their muskets. . . .

The confidence that a sight of the fighting material of Johnston's army helped to restore to Richmond was strengthened somewhat, in that returning spring of 1862, by the knowledge that the city at last was fortified. . . . **page 68/** Richmond, of course, did not read these reports [secret reports which told of the feebleness of the armament]. The city saw only that the batteries had been erected and in them Richmond felt a certain security, a security that swift events threatened, by a succession of new disasters, to bring to a test. On April 25, the South shuddered to hear that New Orleans had fallen. . . .

On Sunday, May 4, when Richmonders finished church services, they were startled to hear that sick soldiers had arrived from Yorktown via West Point and had reported that General Johnston's army had evacuated that position. The next day brought rumor and Tuesday brought confirmation of a rearguard action at Williamsburg. Confederate soldiers had fought with a gallantry expected of them, but they had been forced to leave their wounded on the field. Johnston's army was in retreat . . . with the Chickahominy as the next defensive line. A week of anxiety began, the fearful left Richmond in trainloads. Doubt was expressed whether an attempt would be made to defend the city. Archives were packed up.

Although the President had told all inquirers that he intended to defend Richmond, a new panic began when it became known that he had sent his own family to a place of safety. Many well-to-do persons took the first cars southward and arrived in North Carolina towns with little more than the clothes on their backs.

At 7:45 on the morning of May 15, 1862, as leisured Richmonders were eating breakfast, they stopped and listened to a sudden distant rumble. . . .

There was no mistaking it. Although Richmonders had never heard hostile guns, or even friendly cannon except on salute or practice, the city knew what that sound meant: the enemy was in the river. . . . If the Confederates **page 72/** beat off the attack, the city was safe; but if the Federals passed the fort and the obstructions. . . .

.　.　.　.　.　.　.

As the women went indoors to pray, the men gravitated to the Capitol Square and thence to the City Hall. The despair and panic of previous days suddenly vanished. Now that danger was near and the Federals actually were attacking the defenses of the city, courage rose to determination.

.　.　.　.　.　.　.

At 11:05 A.M. as if the enemy despaired at taking so gallant a city, the firing fell away. In a few minutes it stopped. After three hours' roar, the wonted silence of the city seemed strange . . . And then the news came: the enemy's squadron had been defeated. . . . **page 73/**

A month and a half from the day Richmond had heard the opening salvo in the attack on Drewry's Bluff, the immediate danger was past. The second great march on Richmond [McClellan's Peninsula Campaign] had been thwarted as completely as that which had ended at Manassas the previous summer.

.　.　.　.　.　.　.

Richmond now knew what a monstrous price the South had to pay for victories which bombastic spell-binders had said in the spring of 1861 would carry the Southern army into Washington after the first clash. Something of the ghastliness of war-wounds had been revealed when the boys who had fallen on the plains of Manassas had been brought to Richmond. Their number, however, had not exceeded the city's ability to nurse them.

. . . . . .

The combined capacity of all Confederate hospitals in Richmond; military and private, in the late winter of 1861-62, is said to have been 2,500. . . . . All together, there were 9,000 sick when General Johnston determined to evacuate the Manassas line. [The great majority of the soldiers came from rural districts and had never passed through the familiar children's diseases.]

General Johnston accordingly notified the War Department that those 9,000 sick would be sent south of the Rappahanock, the greatest number to Richmond. Never had such a call been made and never had one of such magnitude even been antici-pated. How, conceivably, could a city of 38,000, crowded already to more than double its housing capacity, find beds for 9,000 men?   page 74/

. . . . . .

Chimborazo [an amazingly-efficiently run hospital which was constructed to meet the needs] and the other hospitals were able to care for the wounded that General Johnston removed from Manassas. When the ghastly battles of 1862 and 1863 were fought, the wounded were sent to Richmond whenever their condition and the available transport permitted. Under the act of September 27, 1862, hos-pitals in Richmond and in other centers of medical service were assigned numbers and, in addition, were designated by State names so that the men from a given State, in sickness, pain, or death, would be attended by surgeons and would be surrounded by men and matrons of their own soil.

Visitation of one or another of these hospitals was part of the duty of every Richmond woman who could endure the strain on her emotions. In a great emer-gency, such as that presented by the Battle of Seven Pines, which occurred before the hospitals had been expanded adequately, private homes were thrown open.

. . . . . .

Not all the experiences of women in the hospitals of Richmond and of other cities were gruesome. On occasion, the lightly wounded soldiers were humorous and not a little bored at the attention given them. One of the favorite stories of the times — attributed to almost every war-time hospital of the Confederacy — had to do with the veteran whom a tender-hearted young woman approached with the inquiry, "Can't I do something for you, sir?"

"No thank you, ma'am."

"Is there nothing?"

"No thank you, ma'am."

"Can't I wash your face for you?"

"Well, if you insist, ma'am, all right, but fourteen ladies have washed it already today."

. . . . . .

. . . All in all it was reasonable to say that admissions to the Confederate military hospitals in Richmond during the war ran above 175,000 and may have reached 200,000. The dead in this vast army fill most of the graves in the soldiers' sections at Oakwood and at Hollywood. Before the war Oakwood was a small cemetery.

When the war ended it was something more than a euphemism, a "city of the dead."
page 75/

.   .   .   .

For every woman in Richmond who was willing to do dangerous manual work, the munitions plants offered regular employment. Gorgas' [Josiah Gorgas, Chief of Ordnance] admirable system reduced accidents, but explosions sometimes occurred in the loading rooms. In the worst of these, a number of girls and women were killed. Their fellow-workers, some 500 wives, mothers, and sisters of soldiers, went back to work as diligently as before.

.   .   .   .

[The Confederacy] never had commanded the full support of all the people. Even in Richmond, which was as loyal as any city of the South, there had been an undercurrent of resistance to the cause. After the disaster at Roanoke Island, it was not unusual to see scrawled on Richmond walls, "Union Men to the Rescue" or "God Bless the Stars and Stripes" or such a forewarning of the twentieth century as "Providence has forsaken its pinks!" Many did lip-service to the Confederacy when their patriotism was only that of the pocket. Extortion was unabashed. Efforts were made to "corner" even such necessities as salt. The City Council had to put the municipality into business to purchase and ration salt, meal, and for a time, even fuel. Virginia sold clothes to the naked. Gamblers fattened on the poor pay of officers and men.

The decline of morale is one of the most instructive and monitory lessons in the history of war, as well as some of the most complicated and tragic. . . . The Confederate Capital, oft-beleaguered, oft-delivered, for a long time had believed the Army of Northern Virginia invincible.

Richmond mothers of sure mould confidently had sung their children to sleep while guns had growled. Old clothes had been turned and made over when new garments no longer could be purchased. Courageous girls looked no less lovely because they dressed in calico instead of silk. They danced as gracefully at "starvation parties" as ever they had at great levees.

.   .   .   .

Although the whistles blew and the smoke rose from the arsenal stacks and the women still thronged across the bridge to Byrd Island [the site of the ordinance factories], there was little iron for shells, and less lead for bullets, and almost no copper for caps.

. . . despite the promise of spring, flour was selling for $1500 a barrel, meal for $140 a bushel and bacon for $20 a pound. The city must fall or starve — the only question was which would come first.   **page 78/**

No. 14   Sallie A. Brock Putnam, *Richmond During the War*, New York, G. W. Carleton and Company, 1867.

. . . with the incoming of the Confederate Government, Richmond was flooded with pernicious characters. The population was very soon doubled. Speculators, gamblers, and bad characters of every grade flocked to the capital, and with a lawlessness which for a time bade defiance to authority, pursued the rounds of their wicked professions, and grew rich upon their dishonest gains. Thieving, garrotting, and murdering were the nightly employments of the villains who prowled around the city, until, by the increased vigilance of the police under the newly-appointed Provost Marshal, this alarming state of affairs was in a measure rectified.   **page 76/**

No. 15   Robert Underwood Johnson and Clarence Clough Buel (eds.), *Battles and Leaders of the Civil War*, New York, The Century Company, 1887, vol. 1. (4 vols.).

The Confederate Government at Montgomery

R. BARNWELL RHETT
(Editor of the Charleston *Mercury*, 1860-62)

Of the debates of that body [The Provisional Congress] there is no record, and the proceedings in secret session have never been published. In Washington the proceedings of the Congress of the United States were open, and at the North there was an intelligent, well-informed, powerful public opinion throughout the war. Not so at the South. Secret sessions were commenced at Montgomery, and at Richmond almost all important business was transacted away from the knowledge and thus beyond the criticism of the people. . . . During the war scarcely anything was known except results, and when the war terminated, the people of the South, though greatly dissatisfied, were generally as ignorant of the management of the Confederate affairs as the people of the North. . . . It very well suits men at the South who opposed secession to compliment their own sagacity by assuming that the end was inevitable. Nor do men identified with the Confederacy by office, or feeling obligation for its appreciation of their personal merits, find it hard to persuade themselves that all was done that could be done in the 'lost cause.' And, in general, **page 99/**   it may be an agreeable sop to Southern pride to take for granted that superior numbers alone effected the result. Yet, in the great wars of the world, nothing is so little proved as that the more numerous always and necessarily prevail. On the contrary, the facts of history show that brains have ever been more potent than brawn. The career of the Confederate States exhibits no exception to this rule. Eliminate the good sense and unselfish earnestness of Mr. Lincoln, and the great ability and practical energy of Seward and Adams, and of Stanton and Chase from the control of the affairs of the United States; conceive a management of third-rate and incompetent men in their places — will any one doubt that matters would have ended differently? To many it may be unpalatable to hear that at the South all was not done that might have been done and that cardinal blunders were made. But what is pleasing is not always true, and there can be no good excuse now for suppressing important facts or perverting history.   **page 100/**

. . . a majority of the delegation were opposed to Mr. Davis, but that, not having compared opinions, they did not understand one another, and Mr. Davis received the vote of South Carolina, and was elected, by the casting vote of Mr. Rhett [writer's father]. Personally, Mr. Rhett knew little of Mr. Davis. He regarded him as an accomplished man, but egotistical, arrogant, and vindictive, without depth of statesmanship. Besides this he judged him not sufficiently in accord with the movement to lead it.   **page 102/**

. . . .

In April, 1865, after the collapse of the Confederacy, Mr. Barnwell [the writer's father's second cousin] who had steadfastly supported Mr. Davis in the Confederate Senate, met the writer at Greenville, S.C., where Governor Magrath had summoned the legislature of the state to assemble. There, in conversation, Mr. Barnwell explicitly expressed his judgment in the following words: 'Mr. Davis never had any policy; he drifted, from the beginning to the end of the war.'   **page 110/**

No. 16   Sallie A. Brock Putnam, *Richmond During the War,* New York, G. W. Carleton and Company, 1867.

The administration of Mr. Davis was never wholly acceptable to the people. The nearly arbitrary power conferred upon him placed in his hands almost exclusive control of our military affairs, which were managed in such a way as to irritate some of our most accomplished and best informed generals. His refusal to concede anything to the people in their wishes in regard to changes in the cabinet, to whom, from seeming inefficiency, Mr. Mallory, Secretary of the Navy, and Mr. Benjamin, Secretary of War, had become exceptionable, was the fruitful source of unpopularity. That he made mistakes we all must admit. But the question is — who, in the trying position of ex-President Davis, would have done better? — who as well? He had been charged by some of using his office to put down and elevate whom he chose. Perhaps so. We are not prepared to censure him. General Randolph of Virginia was appointed to fill the vacancy in the War Department, an appointment that was immensely popular, and under which success once more dawned upon the Confederate arms. About the same time the confidence of the people was strengthened by the appointment of General Robert E. Lee by the Confederate Congress to the position of commanding general — a rank created by the demands of our position, and which after being vetoed by the President, was afterwards consented to, **page 108/**   but so modified by him that General Lee as commanding general should "act under his direction."   **page 109/**

No. 17   George Cary Eggleston, *A Rebel's Recollections,* New York, G. P. Putnam's Sons, 1905.

Throughout the management of affairs in Richmond a cumbrous inefficiency was everywhere manifest. From the president, who insulted his premier for presuming to offer some advice about the conduct of the war, and quarreled with his generals because they failed to see the wisdom of the military movement suggested by himself, down to the pettiest clerk in a bureau, there was everywhere a morbid sensitiveness on the subject of personal dignity, and an exaggerated regard for routine, which seriously impaired the efficiency of the government and greatly annoyed the army. Under all the circumstances the reader will not be surprised to learn that the government at Richmond was by no means idolized by the men in the field.   **page 222/**

No. 18   Alfred Hoyt Bill, *The Beleaguered City*, New York, Alfred A. Knopf, 1946.

The Cabinet offered a rich field to carpers. Toombs, the Secretary of State, had resigned in July [1861] to take command of a brigade of Georgia troops on the Virginia front. A violent man and a hard drinker, he was not one to dissemble the disgust with government policies that had led him to do so. Of the Secretary of War it was said late in July that if Heaven would send the Confederacy a Napoleon, "Walker would not give him a commission." And when Attorney General Benjamin, who assumed the War portfolio temporarily, sent Beauregard to take command in the West, Vice President Stephens, Toombs, and General Joseph Johnston were leading critics of the order. The department under the direction of Postmaster General Reagan made a poor showing in comparison with the Federal postal service, which ceased to function in the Confederacy on May 31, 1861. As for Mr. Memminger,   **page 93/**   the Secretary of the Treasury, the well informed heard with amazement of his promise to pay the interest on the government's bonds in specie, for which he must pay a premium in treasury notes at par.

But of the sniping fire of blame and disparagement the President was the real target, and not unjustly so. His cabinet had been of his choosing, and he had been singularly free to choose. Their policies were his, and, excepting the revival of the slave trade, he had succeeded in fastening upon his government every one of the policies he had advocated. The criticism of him descended to personalities, to trivialities; his "quick, pettish manner" in dealing with subordinates, his becoming "less accessible" than formerly, the fact that he was not seen so often on the streets, though he kept up his afternoon rides, and the fact that Mrs. Davis did no work among the wounded as other ladies did, because he feared that her presence in the hospital would impose an unwelcomed restraint. Even his regular attendance at Sunday morning worship at St. Paul's did not escape the adverse notice of War Department clerks when they were called upon to work on Sunday. Small allowance was made for his severe illness in the autumn [1861], for his occasional attacks of ague and seasons of tormenting pain in his blind eye. **page 94/**

No. 19 George Cary Eggleston, *A Rebel's Recollections*, New York, G. P. Putnam's Sons, 1905.

The history of the Confederacy, when it shall be fully written, will appear the story of a dream to those who shall read it, and there are parts of it at least which already seem a nightmare to those of us who helped make it. Founded upon a constitution which jealously withheld from it nearly all the powers of government, without even the poor privilege of existing beyond the moment when some one of the States composing it should see fit to put it to death, the Richmond government nevertheless grew speedily into a despotism, and for four years wielded absolute power over an obedient and uncomplaining people. It tolerated no questioning, brooked no resistance, listened to no remonstrance. **page 193/** It levied taxes of an extraordinary kind upon a people already impoverished almost to the point of starvation. It made of every man a soldier, and extended indefinitely every man's term of enlistment. Under pretense of enforcing the conscription law it established an oppressive system of domiciliary visits. To preserve order and prevent desertion it instituted and maintained a system of guards and passports, not less obnoxious, certainly, than the worst thing of the sort ever devised by the most paternal of despotisms. In short, a government constitutionally weak beyond all precedent was able for four years to exercise in a particularly offensive way all the powers of absolutism, and that, too, over a people who had been living under republican rule for generations. That such a thing was possible seems at the first glance a marvel, but the reasons for it are not far to seek. Despotisms usually ground themselves upon theories of extreme democracy, for one **page 194/** thing, and in this case the consciousness of the power to dissolve and destroy the government at will made the people tolerant of its encroachments upon personal and State rights; the more especially, as the presiding genius of the despotism was the man who had refused a promotion to the rank of brigadier-general of volunteers during the Mexican War, on the ground that the general government could not grant such a commission without violating the rights of a State. The despotism of a government presided over by a man so devoted as he was to State rights seemed less dangerous than it might otherwise have appeared. His theory was so excellent that people pardoned his practice. **page 195/**

No. 20 *Daily Richmond Examiner,* June 1, 1861, p. 3.

Who'll Help to Defend the City?

His Honor, the Mayor, has made several appeals to the citizens for assistance to work on the defenses around the city, but more need is yet required, and we hope our citizens will at once respond. If any of them have any Negroes out of work, or digging implements, or wheel barrows, they will do the patriotic by reporting the same to either the Mayor or to T. H. Wynne, L. W. Glazebrook or N. B. Hill, who compose the committee, and have this matter in charge.

No. 21   Daily Richmond Examiner, June 1, 1861, p. 3.

Strawberries are said to be more plentiful this season than has been known to be the case for many years. We suppose this fact is owing to the blockade fleet in James river, which prevents this luxury from finding its way to Northern ports.

No. 22   William Howard Russell, *My Diary North and South,* London, Bradbury and Evans, 1863, vol. I (2 vols.).

June 2, 1861: But Southern faith is indomitable. With their faithful negroes to raise their corn, sugar, and cotton, whilst their young men are at the wars; with France and England to pour gold into their lap with which to purchase all they need in the contest, they believe they can beat all the powers of the Northern world in arms. Illimitable fields, tilled by multitudinous negroes, open on their sight, and they behold the empires of Europe, with their manufactures, their industry, and their wealth, prostrate at the base of their throne, crying out, "Cotton! More cotton! That is all we ask!"

     Mr. Forstall [an able financier and economist] maintains the South can raise an enormous revenue by a small direct taxation; whilst the North, deprived of Southern resources, will refuse to pay taxes at all, and will accumulate enormous debts, inevitably leading to its financial ruin. He, like every Southern man I have as yet met, expresses unbounded confidence in Mr. Jefferson Davis. I am asked **page 376/** invariably, as the second question from a stranger, "Have you seen our President, sir? don't you think him a very able man?" This unanimity in the estimate of his character, and universal confidence in the head of the State, will prove of incalculable value in a civil war. **page 377/**

No. 23   Richmond *Daily Whig,* June 7, 1861, p. 3.

Richmond's Contribution

About thirty companies of infantry, artillery, and cavalry have been organized in this city, and mustered into the service of the State. At an average of ninety to a company, this would make the number of volunteers sent from Richmond, about

2,700 which is doing very well for a voting population of 4,000. The enrollment of volunteers still continues, and if it becomes necessary, every man in Richmond capable of bearing arms will go forth to aid in repelling the Barbarians of the North.

No. 24 Richmond *Daily Whig*, June 18, 1861, p. 3.

A Water Panic

No little commotion was produced among the residents of Shockoe Hill, yesterday afternoon, by the circulation of a report that the water in the reservoir had been poisoned. Persons solicitous for the physical welfare of friends and neighbors sent messengers post haste, in every direction, to put them on their guard, and we have no doubt that in an hour's time hundreds of men, women, and children, who had swallowed hydrant water during the day, were led to believe the imaginary symptoms that it was "all over with them." The report was not entitled to the slightest credency. The reservoir is and has been, for some length of time, guarded day and night, by armed police; and it must be remembered, moreover, that a very large quantity of poison would be required to impregnate ten millions of gallons of water, that being the usual quantity in the reservoir. It is unnecessary, however, to present any argument to disprove the foolish report, for we state on the authority of Mr. Davis, Superintendent of the Water Works, that there is not the slightest foundation for any such report.

We hope that the Mayor, or Council, will make some effort to discover the individual who started the report, in order that he may be exposed and punished. Hanging would not be a retribution too severe.

No. 25 John B. Jones, *A Rebel War Clerk's Diary*, New York, Old Hickory Bookshop, 1935, vol. I (2 vols.).

June 24, 1861: I must get more lucrative employment, or find something for my son to do. The boarding of my family, alone, goes to more than my salary; and the cost of everything is increasing. **page 55/** [Jones was earning approximately $1100.]

No. 26 *Daily Richmond Examiner*, June 28, 1861, p. 3.

One Way to Open a Grocery

On Wednesday night last, Mr. Fink, who keeps a small establishment on the corner of Broad and Madison Streets, had his window incontinently staved in and his premises invaded by a dashing and gallant band of soldiers, in search of the now apparently almost ubiquitous whiskey. . . .

No. 27   Richmond *Daily Whig,* July 4, 1861, p. 3.

The Fourth of July

As this day is the anniversary of the Declaration of Independence — the great example of *Secession* on the part of our ancestors, which their descendants of the present day have nobly followed — it will doubtless be observed in a quiet way by the people of this city. There may be a few pic-nic excursions, but otherwise, there will be no jubilant celebration of the day. The once popular airs, which we were accustomed to hear on "Independence Day" have been superseded by tunes more inspiring to the Southern heart, for hereafter —

> The Star Spangled Banner, in disgrace shall wave
> O'er the land of the tyrant, and the home of the knave.

No. 28   Alfred Hoyt Bill, *The Beleaguered City,* New York, Alfred A. Knopf, 1946.

The President's answer [to complaints about the disastrous campaign in the "West Virginia" mountains in July, 1861] was to recall General Lee from his mission in western Virginia and charge him with the fortifica-   **page 76/**   tion and defense of the coast of the Southern Atlantic states. The campaign in the mountains had been a dismal failure almost equal to that of the Manassas success. Hardship, exposure, and inadequate rations had caused greater losses than the fighting. Lee came back to Richmond a changed man in appearance and sadly diminished in reputation. The troops had been poor, supplies and equipment worse, and the commanders worst of all. Lee was never at his best in dealing with stubborn subordinates; it would have taken a man of far tougher fiber than his to enforce co-operation between two generals from civil life, Floyd, who had been Buchanan's Secretary of War, and Wise, Virginia's former governor; and Lee's mission had been one of co-ordination rather than command. But on him fell the blame for the failure. In certain quarters he was now spoken of as "Grannie" Lee, and the opinion prevailed that he was a better soldier at a desk than in the field. The *Examiner* noted his departure for the South with the expression of the hope that he would be more successful with the spade than he had been with the sword.

He had so far yielded to the exigencies of rough campaigning as to grow a beard, which his women friends deplored. "Does any one really know Lee?" one woman asked herself at this time. "He looks so cold, quiet and grand." But a War Department clerk thought he could read in the General's face signs of discouragement at the way things were going.   **page 77/**

No. 29 Alfred Hoyt Bill, *The Beleaguered City*, New York, Alfred A. Knopf, 1946.

Lee's position was now [summer of 1861] that of military adviser to the President, who suffered from an exaggerated estimate of his own military ability. After all, was he not a West Pointer? Had not his military career been a distinguished one? Had he not made great improvements in the army of the United States when he was Secretary of War? Had he not been made commander-in-chief of the forces of the "Republic of Mississippi" just before he was called to be President of the Confederacy?   **page 58/** He acted as his own chief of staff, and Lee's status was definitely that of his assistant.   **page 59/**

No. 30   Richmond *Daily Whig*, July 16, 1861, p. 3.

Dogs

The "canines" are becoming quite too numerous in and around Richmond. In quiet times, the dog catchers would have been out ere now. Until they again go their rounds, the complaints of citizens, who are annoyed by the yelping and baying of the curs, will be unceasing.

No. 31   Richmond *Daily Whig*, July 19, 1861, p. 3.

Richmond Markets

. . . Bacon has advanced . . ., the supply inadequate for the demand. Butter is also higher with a brisk demand from all the Atlantic ports as far down as New Orleans. . . . We can discover no signs of any disposition to purchase, for the present, and very little to sell. The stock of provisions is so nearly exhausted that it is unnecessary to give quotations.

No. 32   John B. Jones, *A Rebel War Clerk's Diary*, New York, Old Hickory Bookshop, 1935, vol. I (2 vols.).

July 21, 1861: Mrs. D.[avis] had just got a dispatch from the President announcing a dearly-bought but glorious victory [First Manassas]. Some of the editors of the papers being present, and applying to me for a copy of the dispatch, Mr. Benjamin said he could repeat it from memory, which he did, and I wrote it down for the press. Then joy ruled the hour! The city seemed lifted up, and every one appeared to walk on air. Mr. Hunter's face grew shorter; Mr. Reagan's eyes subsided into their natural size; and Mr. Benjamin's glowed something like Daniel Webstre's [sic] after taking a pint of brandy. The men in place felt that now they held their offices for life, as the *permanent* government would soon be ratified by the people, and that the Rubicon had been passed in earnest. We had gained a great victory; and no doubt existed that it would be followed up the next day. If so, the Federal city would inevitably fall into our hands; and this would soon be followed by the expulsion of the enemy from Southern soil. All men seemed to think that the tide of war would roll from that city northward into the enemy's country, until we should win a glorious peace. **page 65/**

No. 33   Varina Howell Davis, *Jefferson Davis,* New York, Belford Company, 1890, vol. II (2 vols.).

On my first introduction to the ladies of Richmond, I was impressed by the simplicity and sincerity of their manners, their beauty, and the absence of the glaze acquired by association in the merely "fashionable society." They felt the dignity attached to personally conducting their households in the best and most economical manner, cared little for fashionable small-talk, but were full of enthusiasm for their own people, and considered wisely and answered clearly any practical question which would tend to promote the good of their families or their country.

I was impressed by a certain offishness in their manner toward strangers; they seemed to feel that an inundation of people perhaps   **page 202/** of doubtful standards, and, at best, of different methods, had poured over the city, and they reserved their judgment and confidence, while they preferred a large hospitality. It was the manner usually found in English society toward strangers, no matter how well introduced, a wary welcome. In the more southern and less thickly settled part of our country, we had frontier hospitality because it was a necessity of the case. In Virginia, where the distances were not so great, and the candidates for entertainment were more numerous, it was of necessity more restricted. **page 203/**

No. 34   Sallie A. Brock Putnam, *Richmond During the War,* New York, G. W. Carleton and Company, 1867.

. . . If our hospital accommodations for the sick and the wounded of our own army were inadequate, we may surely be pardoned for not having comfortable accommodations for the   **page 65/** prisoners. Tobacco warehouses and other buildings used for similar purposes had to be made the receptacles for the men taken captive at that time [First Manassas]; and if, as too surely must have been the case, they proved unfitted and insufficient in size to accommodate with any sort of comfort the many crowded in, by the exigencies of their singular appearance among us, it was simply because at that time no other disposition could be made of them, and surely with no design or desire to inflict useless and cowardly torture on unarmed men, who, as prisoners of war, by all the rules of honor are entitled to due consideration as such. Any positive violation of these duties, is a violation of the holiest obligations which can exist between nations. Notwithstanding all the odium which is cast upon the Southern people for the maltreatment of prisoners, and the infamy which attaches to the names of Libby Prison and Belle Island, we learn from authority which we cannot permit ourselves to believe would be guilty of a base prevarication, that, universally, the prisoners confined in those prisons in Richmond received rations always as good as those furnished to our soldiers in the field, and often of superior quality; while the sick and wounded received the usual rations furnished the sick and wounded Confederates in the hospitals. And for the acts of cruelty accredited to the South in the treatment of prisoners, we trust that a generous public will admit the cases were exceptional and not general, and the evidence influenced by sectional feeling.   **page 66/**

No. 35   Richmond *Daily Whig,* July 24, 1861, p. 3.

Providing for the Wounded

The committee appointed at the citizens meeting, Monday afternoon [July 22] to provide for the comfort of the soldiers wounded in the battle of Manassas, were in session, yesterday, concerting and maturing the necessary arrangements. A large number of citizens came forward and proposed to receive the wounded into their homes, as far as they could, respectively, accommodate them — some proposing to take fifteen or twenty, and none less than two. This disposition seems universal among the community. On conference, however, with Dr. DeLeon, Surgeon General of the Confederate Army, it was deemed best to establish a temporary hospital to which the badly wounded could be conveyed and cared for.

.   .   .   .

Accordingly, a sub-committee was appointed to select a suitable place for the hospital. In discharge of this duty the committee fixed upon the St. Charles Hotel, now untenanted, and in the interview with the proprietor, Mr. R. H. Dickinson, that gentleman, with a generosity worthy of the occasion, tendered the use of the Hotel, for the purpose indicated, without charge. . . .

No. 36   Mary Boykin Chesnut, *A Diary from Dixie,* Boston, Houghton Mifflin Company, 1949.

August 1, 1861: If I were to pick out the best-abused man in Richmond, now when all catch it so bountifully, I should say Mr. Commissary General Northrop was the most cursed and villified. He is held accountable for every thing that goes wrong in the army. He may not be efficient, but his having been a classmate and crony of Jeff Davis at West Point points the moral and adorns the tale. I hear that alluded to oftenest of his many crimes. They say Beauregard writes that his army is upon the verge of starvation; and here in Richmond every man, woman and child is ready to hang to the very first lamp post any one of whom the army complains. Every Manassas soldier is a hero, dear to our patriotic hearts. Put up with any neglect of the heroes of the 21st July? Never!

And now they say we did not move on right after the flying foe because we had no provisions, no wagons, no ammunition, and so on. Rain, mud, and Northrop; these restrained us. But then where were the enemy's supplies that we bragged so of bagging? Echo answers where! **page 99/**

No. 37   Richmond *Daily Whig*, August 27, 1861, p. 2.

There are impatient and splenetic individuals, who most imprudently venture to censure the Commander-in-Chief for not taking Washington after Johnston and Beauregard, under his direction, had repulsed the enemy from the field of Manassas. They are quite willing to do him the justice to admit that great credit is due for the selection of proper generals and for the concentration of a sufficient body of troops at the right place — for the timely telegraphic order to Johnston to bring upon the field the reinforcements of four thousand, which really decided the day — and for the electric effect produced by his presence on the field of battle, "when the dying turned their gaze upon him and blessed him, and the wounded returned to the fight" — but still they entertain the unreasonable regret that he did not take Washington City. If we are pleased at what has been accomplished, how can we know that we should not be even better pleased at what has been averted? Who would have it written that, after having gained a hard-fought battle, our weary and wounded soldiers were led to the Potomac; where they were slaughtered by overwhelming numbers, held in reserve, with innumerable batteries deliberately placed to guard every approach to the Federal City. Thus, less prudent, commanders in other countries have had victory snatched from their grasp; and President Davis, mindful of the responsibility resting upon him, involving not only the honor and independence of the Government of which he is the chief magistrate, but our existence as a people, forebore to rush to unnecessary perils. . . .

No. 38   *Daily Richmond Examiner*, August 27, 1861, p. 3.

The county jail is now filled to its utmost capacity, and one over. There are now, of all ages, sexes, nationalities and colours, fifty-one prisoners confined in this institution, and to crowd it more would be downright cruelty. . . .

Too much praise cannot be accorded the superintendent of this prison for the cleanly and comfortable manner in which it is always kept, notwithstanding the crowded condition of all of its wards ever since the breaking out of the present hostilities.

No. 39 Catherine C. Hopley, *Life in the South*, London, Chapman and Hall, 1863, vol. II (2 vols.).

[Miss Hopley was a "Blockaded British Subject" who spent the time from the spring of 1860 to August 1862 in various cities in the South.]

One could not help thinking that if the Northern President could take a peep at Richmond some fine day, he would think he had not yet made much progress toward "subjugating the South." The streets and parks were thronged with cheerful faces, and groups of soldiers everywhere lounging and laughing. Let him peep in at the hotel of an evening and listen to the music and the mirth within, and serenades without. Let him gaze upon the well-stocked tables, and visit the markets, and he would have been inclined to give up the task as hopeless. Above all, let him hear a few sentiments expressed by some of the slaves, and he would find his own toiling, starving poor, more worthy objects of his chivalry.

With the exception of some imported items of food and luxuries, the usual articles of consumption were still abundant; [end of summer, 1861] and the guests at the hotel drank the tepid and muddy water of the James river with great contentment. Iceless, however, it required intense thirst to accomplish this. . . . **page 40/**

No. 40 *Daily Richmond Examiner*, September 6, 1861, p. 3.

Arrival of General Albert S. Johnson [sic]

General Albert S. Johnson [sic], of Kentucky, accompanied by his aide-de-camp, Colonel Thomas Howard, of Texas, reached this city from New Orleans, yesterday afternoon, and took quarters at the Spotswood House. The arrival of the distinguished military chieftain was soon noised about, and many acquaintances and admirers of the General hastened to pay their respects to him, and to congratulate him upon his successful, though arduous, journey from San Francisco to Richmond, a distance of upwards of 2,300 miles. . . . It was the intention of a number of spirited citizens to compliment General Johnson [sic] with a serenade last night.

No. 41 *Daily Richmond Examiner*, September 16, 1861, p. 3.

The city was comparatively quiet yesterday, owing to the closing of the drinking shops. No shooting or stabbing cases were reported by the police. It would be as well, however, for our citizens to keep their front doors locked after night, as there is no knowing what may happen.

No. 42   *Daily Richmond Examiner,* September 19, 1861, p. 3.

The Confederate Reading Room

It affords us a very sincere gratification to be able to announce that the long-standing reproach to Richmond — the want of a well-organized Reading Room — is at length removed. A pleasant and extensive one has just been opened on Eleventh Street, two doors North of Main Street, (within a few steps of the American Hotel) where — in addition to all the city papers — can be found on file, papers from every State, city and town of the South. Strangers from any part of the country, however remote — whether from Virginia or Texas — can find here papers from their homes — as it is principally with this object the Confederate Reading Room was established. Facilities for writing are also at the service of visitors, free of charge. The rates of admission are very low — 10 cents, single admission; 50 cents per month; $5 per annum.

No. 43   *Daily Richmond Examiner,* September 26, 1861, p. 3.

Postage Stamps

The want of this necessary accommodation in Richmond, to which our people have become used under the old Washington Government, is felt to be a most serious inconvenience by all who rely upon the Postal Department of the Confederate Government as a means of communication. In other cities, as is well known, postmasters have issued their own postage stamps, which, while good only for the particular locality whose interest they were designed to subserve, have proved efficient aids in the dispatch of business. The people evince much anxiety to know why similar expedients cannot be adopted here. It seems to be conceded that something ought to be done to allay the growing discontent.

No. 44   Catherine C. Hopley, *Life in the South,* London, Chapman and Hall, 1863, vol. II (2 vols.).

Richmond was the last large city in the Confederacy to issue its own postage stamps. New Orleans, Memphis, Charleston had long ago adopted them, but at Richmond we still prepaid our letters, and in specie too. Everybody was complaining. A friend at Fredericksburg wrote that she had, in September, received a letter written in Richmond on the 22nd of August, and post-marked "Richmond, August 23rd, 1861." "Sixty miles only from Richmond, and yet a letter bearing date August 22, not received here till the 11th of September." **page 66/**

No. 45 *Daily Richmond Examiner,* October 8, 1861, p. 3.

Rapid Driving

The citizens begin to complain loudly of the reckless manner in which the drivers of heavy wagons and other vehicles urge their steeds through our main thoroughfares, which, it is claimed, is now seriously done to the serious annoyance of foot passengers and great prejudice of an unrestricted and safe navigation of the streets. . . .

No. 46 *Daily Richmond Examiner,* October 17, 1861, p. 3.

Some of the gutters in the city need the fostering care of the Street Superintendent. Their offense is rank and smells to heaven, besides poisoning the surrounding atmosphere. . . . The letting loose of the fire plug on the North side of Broad Street, and the running of the water for an hour or two, would conduce much to the purity of the atmosphere in that locality.

No. 47 *Daily Richmond Examiner,* October 19, 1861, p. 3.

Free Schools of Richmond

There are nine free schools in Richmond. Dr. John Dove, who has held the office of Superintendent of the Board of School Commissioners for many years past, reported at the last meeting of the Council that the number of children attending the different schools was 1,326, the average daily attendance of each child 80 days, and the expense to the city for tuition of each, daily, was three cents. The several schools are in a healthy condition.

No. 48 *Daily Richmond Examiner,* November 11, 1861, p. 3.

Descent Upon the Gamblers

On Saturday night a descent was made upon the gamblers in Richmond, and a number of their dens broken up, temporarily, at least, by the arrest of the proprietors and their gambling furniture. The community will be greatly rejoiced to learn that steps have at last been taken to cleanse Richmond of these vile habitations, and to relieve the community of one of its worst moral pests. We are sorry, however, to find that the city authorities have been to the last derelict in any steps to break up the gambling establishments in Richmond, and we understand that the vigorous measures on Saturday night were only undertaken by the Mayor and Police at the urgent insistence of the authorities of the Government. The circumstance is an unfortunate commentary on our municipal rule and dawdling police, who do nothing but hunt belated negroes without passes and hang about the barrooms as impecunious vagabonds. Assuredly the Mayor of Richmond must have been aware of the existence of gambling establishments in this city; for months the evil has been growing openly and defiantly before his eyes; and that, at last, the Government residing here should, from its own considerations of respect and decency, have had to urge the cleansing of the city by instancing the municipal authorities to do their duty, is a circumstance apparently so discreditable to the people of Richmond that justice to them requires that it should be referred to official neglect and omission of duty, rather than imputed to any corrupt moral sense in the community.

No. 49   *Daily Richmond Examiner,* November 18, 1861, p. 1.

Notes of a Recent Tour in the South

[Reprinted from the New York *Herald* of November 12, 1861.]

The principal feature that strikes every one who sees Richmond for the first time is its curious topography. From the James River, which, tumbling over its rocky bed, makes a wide bend here, with its convex face to the city, rise, without any regard to uniformity of direction, some half dozen hills, of gravel formation, and of pretty considerable elevation. There has never been any attempt to grade them into level streets, but the city is scattered promiscuously up and on and over them, just as fashions taste or business may have happened to dictate. The principal part of the city, however, occupies actually one of these elevations, and the garden spot of that one is the Capitol Square, where stands the building of which Jefferson secured the design in France. . . .

Richmond has really but one business thoroughfare. That is Main Street. Most of the hotels, banks, newspaper offices, and stores are located on it. It extends Northward into the open country, and Southward to a suburb called Rocketts. In this latter section of it are situated some of the tobacco warehouses where our Union prisoners are now confined. . . .

Near the summit of the elevation known as Church Hill is a large, old fashioned brick building known as the Alms House. It has been converted from its original purpose, and now serves as an hospital for our sick and wounded. Sisters of Charity come and go, untiring angels of consolation, and the hearse is kept in constant requisition, so great is the mortality that prevails here. . . . On the most commanding part of Church Hill still stands, in good preservation, too, the Church in which Patrick Henry made the famous speech at the commencement of the revolutionary struggle. Around the church are the graves of the last generation of the people of Richmond. . . .

But Richmond is not, as seems erroneously to be considered, garrisoned by a large army. So far as I could see there are only camps of instruction maintained here. . . . One camp of instruction is a level tract of ground between the penitentiary and the new cemetery, which used to be occupied as a fair ground. Another and more extensive one is on the North side of the city, about a mile and a half out on the line of the Fredericksburg railroad, where there is an enclosure about a mile square, sometimes used as a race course. I believe it is called the New Fair Ground. . . . Wherever there is space and eligible ground for camps, it is covered with tents. The soldiers are not allowed quarters in the city, but are kept strictly to their camp-life; but the officers — scions of all the first families — are treated with more consideration, and are allowed to consult their comfort so far as to occupy town quarters. . . . There may be from eight to ten thousand soldiers around Richmond, but these are not regarded, as I said, in the light of a garrison, but only as apprentices, acquiring their initiatory lessons in military life. They are, therefore, kept constantly on the move; those who have the advantage of five or six weeks' training giving place to new hands.

. . . .

In the Western section of the city, on the banks of the James river, is the State Arsenal, a large, substantial, building, where arms are being manufactured. Quite close to it are the Tredegar Iron Works, an extensive concern, which has done nothing since April last except cast cannon and balls for the use of the rebels. . . . On the bluff rising above the Tredegar Works stands the penitentiary, surrounded by a high wall, and some distance back of it is the new cemetery. The level space between is used as a camp of instruction. A little higher up the river, just where the grounds of the cemetery come down, are the Water Works.

Business is generally represented as completely ruined, except those branches of trade that are connected with the equipment and supplies of the army. These are flourishing, but the only currency to be had is paper money; and when the war ends those who have appeared to drive the most thriving business will probably find themselves rich only in worthless "shinplasters." Nevertheless, the people do not seem inclined to look far into the future, and as bank-notes, issued in unlimited supply, and without any regard to corresponding capital, will pass current in trade, these do not appear to be very hard times. Those branches of trade that are connected with articles of luxury, or articles not of the first necessity, are entirely ruined, and many are the empty stores that can be seen in Main Street, silent witnesses against the madness of the hour. Still the sidewalks are crowded with pedestrians and on the whole, Richmond may be said to be a gay city.

No. 50 Sallie A. Brock Putnam, *Richmond During the War*, New York, G. W. Carleton and Company, 1867.

Never before had so sad a Christmas dawned upon us [1861]. Our religious services were not remitted, and the Christmas dinner was plenteous as of old; but in nothing further did it remind us of days gone by. We had neither the heart nor inclination to make the week merry with joyousness when such a sad calamity hovered over us. Nowhere else could the heart have been as constantly oppressed by the heavy load of trouble as in Richmond, and the friendly congratulations of the season were followed by anxious inquiries for dear boys in the field, or husbands or fathers whose presence had ever brought brightness to the domestic hall, and whose footsteps were music to the hearts and ears of those to whom they were so dear. **page 89/**

No. 51   T. C. DeLeon, *Four Years in Rebel Capitals*, Mobile, Alabama, The Gossip Printing Company, 1890.

In the beginning as vast crowds poured into Richmond — each man with a little money and anxious to use it to some advantage — trade put on a new and holiday dress. Old shops were spruced up; old stocks, by aid of brushing and additions, were made to appear quite salable and rapidly ran off. The demand made the meat it fed upon, until stores, shops and booths sprang up in all parts of the city and on all the roads leading into it from the camps. Gradually supplies became more scarce as money became more plenty. The pinch began to be felt by many who had never known it before; and almost everyone, who had any surplus portables, was willing to turn them into money. In this way, those who had anything to sell, for the time, managed to live. But the unfortunates who had only what they needed absolutely, or who were forced to live upon a fixed income, that did not increase in any ratio to the decrease of money, suffered terribly.

These were only too ready to take the fever of speculation; and to buy any small lots of anything whatever that might sell again at a profit. This was the class from which the main body of amateur speculators was recruited. One successful venture led to another and gave added means for it. The clerk, or the soldier, who yesterday cleared his hundred on a little turn in whisky, tomorrow might hope to double it — then reinvest his principal and his profits. It was marvelous how values rose over night. One might buy anything, a lot of flour — a line of fruits — a hogshead of molasses, or a case of boots today, with almost a certainty of nearly doubling his outlay today week.

The ordinary channels of trade became clogged and blocked by its constant increase. Auction houses became the means of brokerage; and their number increased to such an extent that half a dozen red flags at last dotted every block in Main street. And incongruous, indeed, were the mixtures exposed at these sales, as well as in the windows of the smallest shops in Richmond. In the latter, **page 236/** bonnets rested on the sturdy legs of cavalry boots; rolls of ribbon were festooned along the crossed barrel of a rifle and the dingy cotton umbrella; while cartridges, loaves of bread, packages of groceries, gloves, letter paper, packs of cards, prayer-books and canteens, jostled each other in admirable confusion.

At these auctions there was utter want of system. Hogsheads of prime rum would be put up after kegs of spikes; a case of organdies would follow a good cavalry horse; and then might come four second-hand feather-beds and a hundred boarding cutlasses.

But everything soever found a purchaser; some because they were absolutely needed and the buyer dreaded waiting the next week's rise; the majority to sell again in this insane game of money-making.

But varied as were the motives for speculation, the principal ones were bread-stuffs and absolute necessities of life; and while the minor speculators — the amateurs — purchased for *quick* profits — the professional vultures bought for *great* ones and could afford to wait.

The first class reached into every rank of society; the second were principally Yankee residents — caught in Richmond by the war, or remaining for the sole purpose of making it pay — and a small class of the lowest Polish Jews. Ishmaels both, owning no kinship and no country, their sole hope was gain — gain at the cost of reputation and credit themselves — gain even at the cost of torture and starvation to the whole South besides. These it was who could afford to buy in bulk; then aid the rise they knew must come inexorably, by hoarding up great quantities of flour, bacon, beef and salt.

It mattered not for themselves who suffered — who starved. It mattered not if the noble fellows at the front lived on a scant handful of cornmeal per day — if starving men died before the works they were too weak to mount — if ghastly objects in hospital and trench literally perished, while their storehouses burst with food — waiting for a rise! **page 237/**

No. 52 T. C. DeLeon, *Four Years in Rebel Capitals,* Mobile, Alabama, The Gossip Printing Company, 1890.

And with the feeling how valueless was money, came another epidemic — not so widespread, perhaps, as the speculation fever; but equally fatal to those who caught it — the rage for gambling!

Impulsive by nature, living in an atmosphere of constant and increasing artificial excitement, feeling that the money worth little today, perhaps, would be worth nothing tomorrow — these men of the South gambled heavily, recklessly and openly. There was no shame — little concealment about it. The money was theirs, they argued, and mighty hardly earned, too. They were cut off from home ties and home amusements; led the life of dumb beasts in camp; and, when they came to town — ho! for "the tiger."

Whether these reasons be valid or not, such they were. And really to the camp-wearied and battle-worn officer, the saloon of the fashionable Richmond "hell" was a thing of beauty. Its luxurious furniture, soft lights, obsequious servants and lavish store of such wines and liquors and cigars as could be had nowhere else in Dixie — these were only part of the inducement. Excitement did the rest, leaving out utterly the vulgar one of possible gain, so rarely did that obtain. But in these faro-banks collected the leading men, resident and alien, of the Capital. Senators, soldiers and the learned professions sat elbow to elbow, round the generous table that offered the choicest viands money could procure. In the handsome rooms above they puffed fragrant Havanas, while the latest developments of news, strategy and policy were discussed; sometimes ably, sometimes flippantly, but always freshly. Here men who had been riding raids in the mountains of the West; had lain shut up in the water batteries of the Mississippi; or had faced the advance of the many "On-to-Richmonds" — met after long separation. Here the wondering young cadet would look first upon some noted raider, or some gallant brigadier — cool and invincible amid the rattle of Minié-balls, as reckless but conquerable amid the rattle of ivory chips.

So the faro-banks flourished and the gamblers waxed fat like   **page 238/** Jeshurun, the ass, and kicked never so boldly at the conscript man. Nor were they all of ignoble memory. There is more than one "sport" in the South today, who made warm and real friends of high position from his acts of real generosity then. **page 239/**

No. 53   T. C. DeLeon, *Belles, Beaux and Brains of the '60's*, New York, G. W. Dillingham Company, 1909.

. . . while the fortune and the larders lasted, the entertainments in Richmond were generous; when the direst constriction of the blockade crushed, the elegance remained, over the crust and the yellow water.

The thought of no habitue of Richmond society of that day can recur to it without being peopled with bright memories of men and women, since famous in the history and society of the Union. Whatever his tastes, business shadowed or pleasure tinted, they doubtless bear borrowed coloring from an era of storm and stress that left its impress deep on all natures, at a moment when most receptive by absorption in a common effort to one great end. The fate of a nation hung in the balance, but the hearts of its integers were hopeful, buoyant and sometimes giddy.

Dinners, dances, receptions and constant visiting followed the earlier arrival of the new government and its Joseph-coated following. There were drives and picnics for the young and, for aught I know to the contrary, much flirtation. The dizzy whirled in recurrent germans, and the buzz of the society bee was heard in the pinkest-tinted ears.

But besides the regular society routine of the capital, much like that in many another city, there was another sociality, quieter, but nowise less attractive to the incoming.   **page 62/**   There were sewing circles, at which the assistants enjoyed the talk of brainy and refined women and cultured men; there music, improvisation and even dancing filled intervals of busy work.

As Dickens made his *Madame Defarge* "knit shrouds" before the greedy knife of the Terror, the sewing circles of Richmond stitched love and hope and sentiment into the rough seams and hems of nondescript garments they sent to the camps by bales. No lint was scraped for wounds to come that was not saturated with pity and tenderness; and the amateur cooks kneaded their hearts into the short piecrust and not always heavy biscuits for "those dear boys."

There were many, and some really excellent amateur concerts, charades and tableaux, by the most modest and sometimes most ambitious amateurs, all for the same good end. And through all of them passed the procession of stately forms and bright faces. On the joggling board of improvised stage, voices that had rung sonorous in the van of battle lisped the sugared nothings of society comedy to Chloes, who later gave the key to society in many a *post-bellum* city. Comic recitations were made by men who have since held listening senates, and verses were penned by women who have now impressed their names on the literature of a time.

Most of this was naturally in the *entr'acte* of war's red **page 63/** drama, in the days of winter's enforced truce, from roads belt-deep in mire or frozen impassable. There were nights when hard-riding Fitz Lee was pressed to pose in tableaux, or dashing "Jeb" Stuart took minor part in a small comedy, to brighten the eyes nearest but not the dearest, for that cause alone.

Of course the storm center of general society was about the presidential household and its actions.

In that dwelling the most weighty and eventful matters of the government had birth and were matured, and there the tireless worker, to himself the Confederacy incarnate, devoted all the days and most of the midnights, planning, considering, changing. The executive officers were elsewhere, but at that day Mr. Davis carried the government in his own brain, and that never slept.

His wildest admirer has never claimed that Jefferson Davis was a saint; his vilest vituperator has never proved him a devil. History shows no man who has faced such fierce and sweeping blasts of indictment, calumny and malice and so long stood erect: a mark inviting scrutiny, but not shrinking beneath it. It is simple truth that his name is today mentioned with respect, or praise, in the capital of every civilized country on the globe, save one, and there the cause of silence or of old-time iteration is more political than judicial.

I am not planting seed for the future Macaulay, but it may be noted here that this absolute self-reliance was one cause of failure; he failed because he could not make the Confederacy Jefferson Davis. The *non sequitur* is often more logical than the epigram. When Sir Boyle Roche said: "No man can be in two places at once, barrin' he's a bird!" he was probably ignorant that he was double-barreled — talking nonsense and philosophy. He did not know that he was laying down a rule of procedure which, persistently **page 64/** deviated from, must result in disaster. That disaster followed was not Mr. Davis's fault. In an article of the *North American Review,* a dozen years ago, I showed that he was not only the president, but that he shouldered the responsibility for every member of his cabinet. He was the head almost of every distinct bureau, in each department of the government.

But it was not on governmental grounds that social Richmond felt uneasy as to the Davis family in those early days. There was no tinge of personality toward the inmates of the White House; only a nervousness as to that nebulous dweller on the threshold of legislative necessity. There was an undefined dread that the official head would be followed by a nameless, yet most distasteful, surrounding of politics and place seekers. **page 65/**

No. 54 Alfred Hoyt Bill, *The Beleaguered City*, New York, Alfred A. Knopf, 1946.

But of all the minor annoyances of that winter [1861-62] in Richmond the police were perhaps the worst for those whose wealth and position did not insure them against the surveillance of General Winder's men. On July 8th a stout, gray-haired old man had appeared at the War Department and applied to be made a general. He was John Henry Winder, late major, U.S. Army, and the son of that unfortunate Winder whose army had sustained the crushing defeat by the British at Bladensburg in 1814, which certainly made his name not one to conjure with. But he was a son of commanding presence and impressive manner, and, still more to his purpose, had been instructor in tactics at West Point when Jefferson Davis was a cadet there. For there was no surer certification for rank in the Confederate army than to have been at the Military Academy in the President's time, except perhaps a **page 96/** harmonious association with him when he was Secretary of War. . . . Within a month Winder had a general's stars on his collar and the command of the Richmond police.

The force which had been adequate in the good old easygoing days when people had seldom troubled to lock their front doors in the daytime had been all but overwhelmed by the wave of crime that had poured into the city with the arrival of the army and the Confederate government. Winder collected a force of secret-service men and proceeded to deal with it promptly and efficiently. . . . These men, it was asserted, were a mere crew of petty-larceny detectives from Baltimore, Phila-delphia, and New York — low and illiterate plug-uglies who interfered intolerably with citizens going about their lawful business and did nothing to eradicate the system of Federal spies that was believed to be active everywhere.   **page 97/**

No. 55 Sallie A. Brock Putnam, *Richmond During the War*, New York, G. W. Carleton and Company, 1867.

During all this time [winter of 1861-62] extortion had increased in Richmond, until the complaints of the people grew loud and terrible. Articles of food, absolutely necessary to sustain life, had gone up in price, until it was thought a necessity to legislate upon the traffic. General Winder, the Provost Marshal of the city, in order to remedy the evil, laid a tariff of prices on all articles of domestic produce, but did not legislate upon groceries, liquors, and articles imported from abroad.

The consequence was, the markets were so ill supplied that they had almost as well been closed.

It was next to an impossibility to procure a dinner at all. The meats were so indifferent as scarcely to be fit for food, and fish became the staple article. To secure these, it was necessary to send to market for them before the break of day, and frequently, then, the crowd that pressed around the fish-market was so dense that many were compelled to leave without anything for a dinner, except potatoes and poor beef, and the market men declared that people might "starve!" — they would bring in no more supplies until the tariff was withdrawn, or the sale of imported articles regulated in a manner to protect *them* likewise from imposition. They argued, if they were forced to pay the exorbitant demands for sugar, tea, brandy, and other articles from abroad, they had a right to charge similar prices for their meats, poultry, butter and vegetables, or they would not sell them. The greatest inconvenience arose from the want of such articles of food as were in the power of hucksters to control. Butter and eggs were never seen, and the fishmongers grew tired of the annoyances to which they were continually subjected by their hungry patrons, and refused to keep up a supply.

Finding our situation so deplorable, and soliciting relief, through a committee of citizens appointed to wait upon the page 113/ Provost Marshal, the tariff was raised, and the merchandise of the hucksters again flowed into our markets. From that time until the end of the war we were entirely at their mercy. Being wholly dependent upon them for so much that was essential for existence, they charged what prices they pleased for their merchandise, and we were forced to pay them or abstain from many necessary articles of food altogether. As if to recompense themselves for time and money lost to them while the tariff was enforced by the military authority, they doubled the old prices on their merchandise, and where the people groaned under the extortion before, they found the burden so much increased that the groaning was doubled in proportion. page 114/

No. 56   T. C. DeLeon, *Belles, Beaux and Brains of the '60's*, New York, G. W. Dillingham Company, 1909.

What came nearest to a salon in Richmond — and, as far as I know in all America — was held at Mrs. Robert C. Stanard's. Her home early became noted for hospitality as lavish as it was elegant. She was a widow of ample means, and had been Miss Martha Pierce, of Louisville. She courted social success, had traveled extensively, and made many and distinguished friends.

When stress of war mobilized an army of these in Richmond, Mrs. Stanard's doors swung wide and early for their reception and refection. She was one of the very first to break that thin layer of ice over the home society which formed at first hint of the white frost of social invasion, and for a moment threatened to chill the dreaded unknown.

It has been shown how the natural warmth of Virginian hospitality soon dissipated this premature film; and how the natural sunniness of Richmond nature returned and rose to higher degree than normal. This desideratum was due to practical people like Mrs. Stanard, who had known some of the incoming and were ready to take the whole crop, as the cotton buyer does, "by sample." Those who met the best of the influx at such houses, early "went in and bulled the foreign market."

At her frequent dinners, receptions and evenings, Mrs. Stanard collected most that was brilliant and brainiest in government, army, congress and the few families who followed either, apparently because they could afford to.

There one met statesmen like Lamar, Benjamin, Pierre Soulé **page 198/** and their peers; jurists like John A. Campbell and Thomas J. Semmes; fighters like Johnson, Hampton, and Gordon; and the most polished and promising of the youth of war, as gallant and classic Kyd Douglas, handsome John B. Castleman, Lord King and a host more, not to name all of whom seems invidious. And with these came the best of her own sex that the tact and experience of the hostess could select.

Bref, at Mrs. Stanard's one met people already noted for something — or were sure to be ere long. Her house was one unremittent salon, in the regard of variety; and with the difference that the comers were entertained as well as entertaining. **page 199/**

No. 57   T. C. DeLeon, *Four Years in Rebel Capitals,* Mobile, Alabama, The Gossip Printing Company, 1890.

The novelty most remarked in the society of this winter [1861-62] was the household of President Davis. Soon after the Government was firmly established in Richmond, the State of Virginia placed at his disposal a plain but comfortable house; and here — with only the ladies of his family and his private secretary — he lived with the quiet simplicity of a private citizen.

It will hardly be invading her *sacra privata* to say that the President's lady did everything to remove false ideas that sprung up regarding the social atmosphere of the "Executive Mansion." She was "at home" every evening; and, collecting around her a staff that numbered some of the most noted men and brilliant women both of the stranger and resident society, assured all her varied guests a warm welcome and a pleasant visit. In this circle Mr. Davis would, after the trying business of the day, give himself an hour's relaxation before entering on labors that went far into the night; and favored friends and chance visitors alike here met the man, whence they expected the official.

Austere and thoughtful at all times, rarely unbending to show the vein of humor hidden deep under his stern exterior, and having besides "the divinity that doth hedge" even a republican president, Mr. Davis was never calculated for personal popularity. Even in the early days of his career he forced by his higher qualities — rather than sort by the arts of a trickster — the suffrages of his people; and they continued to cast their shells for him, even while they clamored that he was "the Just."   **page 153/**

No. 58   T. C. DeLeon, *Four Years in Rebel Capitals,* Mobile, Alabama, The Gossip Printing Company, 1890.

While everything was dull and lifeless in the camps of the South [during the winter of 1861-62], a far different aspect was presented by its Capital. There was a stir and a bustle new to Quiet Richmond. Congress had brought crowds of attachés and hangers-on; and every department had its scores of dependents. Officers from all quarters came in crowds to spend a short furlough, or to attend to some points of interest to their commands before the bureaus of the War Department. The full hotels showed activity and life unknown to them. Business houses, attracted by the increased demands of trade and the new channels opened by Government necessities, sprang up on all sides; and the stores — though cramped by the blockade — began to brush off their dust and show their best for the new customers. Every branch of industry seemed to receive fresh impetus; and houses that had for years plodded on it moldy obscurity shot, with the rapidity of Jonah's gourd, up to first-class business.

The streets presented a scene of unwonted activity; and Franklin street — the promenade *par excellence,* vied with "the avenue" in the character and variety of crowds that thronged its pavement. The majority of the promenaders were officers, their uniforms contrasting brightly with the more quiet dresses around. While many of them were strangers, and the peculiarities of every State showed in the faces that passed in rapid panorama, yet numbers of "Richmond Boys" came back for a short holiday; almost every one bringing his laurels and his commission. **page 147/**

. . . .

. . . The people of Richmond had at first held up their hands in holy horror at the mere mention of amusement! What! with a war in the land must people enjoy themselves? Never! it would be heartless!

But human nature in Virginia is pretty much like human nature everywhere else; and bad as the war was, people gradually got used to the "situation." They had lost friends — a relation or two was pretty badly marked perhaps — but what glory the tens and hundreds left had gained! There was no fighting now; and the poor fellows in camp would be only too glad to know that their brothers-in-arms were being paid for their toils by the smiles of the fair. The great majority of the strangers, too, were young men who had been recommended to the mercy of the society by these very sufferers in camp.

Gradually these influences worked — the younger and gayer people indulged in the "danceable teas," after their sewing circles. Imperceptibly the sewing was left for other times; and by Christmas there was a more constant — if less formal and general — round of gaiety than had been known for years. This brought the citizens and strangers more together, and naturally the result was a long season of more regular parties and unprecedented gaiety. Many still frowned at this, and, as usual, made unhappy Washington the scapegoat — averring that her pernicious example of heartlessness and frivolity had worked the evil.

These rigid Romans staid [sic] at home and worked on zealously in their manufacture of warm clothing, deformed socks and impossible gloves for the soldier boys. All honor to them for their constancy, if they thought they were right, and the harmless gaiety wrong; and they fought the good fight, from behind their *abatis* of knitting needles, only with the innocent weapons of tongue and precept. But human nature and inclination still held their own; and there were many defections from the ranks of the elect, to those of the more practical — and probably equally well-intentioned — pleasure-seekers.   **page 148/**

1862

"Let me whisper: this dress, that I now wear for thee,
*Was a curtain of old, in Philadelphee!"**

---

*Quoted in T. C. DeLeon, *Belles, Beaux and Brains of the '60's*, New York, G. W. Dillingham Company, 1909, p. 396.

No. 59 Virginia Tunstall Clay, *A Belle of the Fifties,* New York, Doubleday, Page and Company, 1905.

Richmond, as seen from the hill, with the James River flowing by, its broad, level streets, full foliaged trees, and spacious homes, is a beautiful city. Rich in historic association, never did it appear more attractive to Southern eyes than when, arriving in the late autumn of '61, we found our Confederate Government established there, and the air full of activity. To accommodate the influx of Congressional and military folk, the houses of the patriotic residents were thrown open until the capacity of every residence, hotel and lodging-house was tested to the fullest. By the time Senator Clay and I arrived, there was scarcely an extra bed to be had in the city, and though everywhere it was apparent that an unsettled feeling existed, there was nothing either indeterminate or volatile in the zeal with which the dense community was fired. As the new-comers, for the greater part, represented families which a season before had been conspicuous in Washington, society was in the most buoyant of spirits. Our courage was high, for our army had won glorious battles against remarkable odds, and, though gallant men had fallen, as occasion demanded them, new heroes sprang to meet it.

For a few months we revelled in canvas-backs and green-backs, undisturbed by forewarnings of coming draw-backs. . . . We feasted on oysters and terrapin of the finest, and unmeasured hospitality was the order of the day on every   **page 168/** side. Never had I looked upon so great an activity, whether military, political, or social.

. . . there were heroes to dine and to cheer in Richmond, both civil and military. . . .

A sororal spirit actuated our women, and while our greatest entertainment missed some of the mere display which had marked the social events in the Federal City, they were happier gatherings, for we were a people united in interest and in heart. Some of the brightest memories I carry of that first session are of informal evenings where neighbors gathered *sans ceremonie.* . . . **page 169/**

During our first winter in Richmond my husband and I made our home with Mrs. Du Val [Mrs. Gabriel], near to the Exchange Hotel, a terrifically over-crowded hostelry at all Confederate times, and within a short walk of the Seddon home, now the Executive Mansion. It was a commodious and stately structure, in which our President, now domiciled, lived with an admirable disdain of display. Statesmen passing through the halls on their way to the discussion of weighty things were likely to hear the ringing laughter of the care-free and happy Davis children issuing from somewhere above stairs or the gardens. The circle at Mrs. Du Val's, our head-quarters, as it came and went for those three eventful years, comprised some of our former Washington mess-mates, and others newly called into public service. Among

the favorites was General J. E. B. Stuart, a rollicking fellow, who loved music, and
page 170/   himself could sing a most pleasing ballad. He was wont to dash up
to the gate on his horse, his plumes waving, and he appearing to our hopeful eyes
a veritable Murat. He was a gallant soldier, what might be termed delightful company, and one of the most daring cavalry officers our service boasted. . . . When
the exigencies of the service brought him again and again to the capital, he entered
heartily into its social relaxations. Two years passed. He was conspicuous one night
in charades, and the next they brought him in, dying from a ghastly wound received
upon the battlefield.

I have said we were in gay spirits during that first session of the Confederate
Congress; but this condition was resolved upon rather than the spontaneous expression of our real mood, though hope was strong and we were armed with a conviction of right upon our side, and with the assurance of the courage of our soldiers,
which filled us with a fine feminine scorn of the mere might of our assailants. Our
editors, filled with patriotism and alert, kept us informed of the stirring events of the
field and of the great victories which, until the loss of Fort Donelson and the fall
of Nashville, so often stood to our credit. Scarcely a triumph, nevertheless, in which
was not borne down some friend who was dear to us, so that all news of victory
gained might be matched with the story of fearful loss. However, such was our
loyalty to the cause, that the stimulus of our victories overbore the sorrow for our
losses, sustaining our courage on every side. Before that first session of Congress
adjourned, we had buried an army of brave men, among them Generals   page 171/
Zollicoffer [Felix K.] and Albert Sidney Johnston. Our coast was closed by the
blockading fleets of the Federal Government. We had lost New Orleans, and the
Tennessee Valley was slipping from us. . . .   page 172/

. . . at the capital the nation's losses and gains loomed large and obscured the
lesser ones of individuals. Moreover, always before us was the stimulus of the
presence of fearless men and the unceasing energy of our President.

I remember on one occasion seeing President Davis passing down the street,
beside him, on the left, General Buckner [Simon B.]; on the right, General Breckenridge [John C.] — three stalwart and gallant men as ever walked abreast; and as
I watched them the thought came involuntarily, "Can a cause fail with such men
at the head?"

Throughout the life of Richmond as a capital, the streets were peopled with
soldiers on their way to and from the several headquarters. There was an uninter-
mitting beating of drums, too often muffled, and the singing of merry bugles. With
the knowledge that we were in the city which, more than any other, invited and
defied the attacks of the enemy, a sense of danger spurred our spirits. Though the
boom of guns was often not a distant sound, and the solemn carrying in of our
wounded became increasingly frequent, few gave way to apprehensions or doubts;
for, as I have said, there were heroes in Richmond to cheer, and our women, putting
away from their minds the remembrance of the wounds they had dressed in the
morning visits to the hospitals, smiled and devised entertainments well calculated
to lift the burden of responsibility, at least for the time being, from the minds and
hearts of our leaders, legislative and military.   page 173/

.   .   .   .

While few, I think, perceived it clearly at that early day, yet in the spring of '62 the fortunes of the Confederacy were declining. Many of our wisest men were already doubtful of the issue even where belief in the justice of our cause never wavered. Looking back upon the prophecies of ultimate defeat that were uttered in those days, by men accustomed to sound the security of governments, I am thrilled at the flood of patriotic feeling on which our men and women were borne to continue in arms against such overwhelming forces and conditions as were brought against them. For months before that first Congress adjourned, from every part of our federated states, eager petitioning, complaints and ominous news reached us. Gold, that universal talisman, was scarce, and Confederate currency began to be looked upon with a doubtful eye. . . .

Within a few months the face of our capital had changed. McClellan's ever-swelling army in the peninsula became more and more menacing. The shadow of **page 178/** coming battles fell over the city, and timid ones hastened away to points that promised more security. Some went to the mountain resorts "to escape the hot term" in Richmond, but many of the wives and daughters of non-house-holders, even among those known to possess a cool courage, moved on to the Carolinas or returned to their native States. As the close of the Congressional session drew near, there was a continual round of good-byes and hand-shakings, and even an attempt now and then at a gaiety which no one actually felt.

Our markets grew suddenly poor, and following quickly upon the heels of a seeming prosperity, a stringency in every department of life in the city was felt. The cost of living was doubled, and, if indeed, any epicures remained, they were glad to put away their fastidiousness. Within a year our vermicelli, when we had it at all, would have warranted an anglicizing of its first two syllables, and our rice, beans, and peas, as well as our store of grains and meal, began to discover a lively interest in their war time surroundings. We heard tales of a lively demand for green persimmons, since a soldier, feeding upon one of these, could feel his stomach draw up and at once forget that he was "hawngry." I remember hearing the story of a certain superficial lady who spoke disdainfully in the hearing of Mrs. Roger A. Pryor, of a barrel of sorghum which some friends had sent her from a distance. Full of contempt, she ordered the offending gift to be taken away. "Horrid stuff!" she said.

"Horrid?" asked Mrs. Pryor, gently. "Why! in these days, with our country in peril, I am grateful when I am able to get a pitcher of sorghum, and I teach my children to thank God for it!"

Our mail, from many quarters, was now become a Pandora's box, from which escaped, as we opened it, myriad apprehensions, dissatisfactions or distresses. . . .
page 179/

No. 60   James D. Richardson, editor, *Messages and Papers of the Confederacy,* Nashville, United States Printing Company, 1905, vol. 1 (2 vols.), p. 220.

General Orders No. 8
Adjutant and Inspector General's Office,
Richmond, March 1, 1862

1. The following proclamation of the President is published for the information of all concerned:

A PROCLAMATION

By virtue of the power vested in me by law to declare the suspension of the privilege of the writ of *habeas corpus* in cities threatened with invasion:

I, Jefferson Davis, President of the Confederate States of America, do proclaim that martial law is hereby extended over the city of Richmond and the adjoining and surrounding country to the distance of ten miles; and I do proclaim the suspension of all civil jurisdiction, with the exception of that of the Mayor of the city, and the suspension of the privilege of the writ of *habeas corpus* within the said city and surrounding country to the distance aforesaid.

In faith whereof, I have hereunto signed my name and set my seal at the [L.S.]   city of Richmond, on this first day of March, in the year one thousand eight hundred and sixty-two.

Jefferson Davis

No. 61   Judith W. McGuire, *Diary of a Southern Refugee,* New York, E. J. Hale & Son, 1867.

March 7, 1862: [The author met with a plain-looking woman in a store.] She was buying Confederate gray cloth, at what   **page 98/**   seemed a high price. I asked her why she did not apply to the quartermaster, and get it cheaper. "Well," she replied, "I *knows* all about that, for my three sons is in the army; they gets their clothes *thar;* but you see this is for my old man, and I don't think it would be fair to get his clothes from *thar,* because he ain't never done nothing for the country as yet — he's just *gwine* in the army." "Is he not very old to go into the army?" "Well, he's fifty-four years old, but he's well and hearty like, and ought to do something for his country. So he says to me, says he, 'The country wants men; I wonder if I could stand marching; I've a great mind to try.' Says I, 'Old man, I don't think you could, you would break down; but I tell you what you can do — you can drive a wagon in the place of a young man that's driving, and the young man can fight.' Says he, 'So I will' — and he's agwine just as soon as I gits these clothes ready, and that won't be long.' " "But won't you be very uneasy about him," I said. "Yes, indeed; but you know he ought to go — them wretches must be drove away." "Did you want your sons to go?" "Want 'em to go!" she exclaimed; "yes; if they hadn't agone, they shouldn't a-staid whar I was. But they wanted to go, *my* sons did." Two days ago I met her again in a baker's shop; she was filling her basket with cakes and pies. "Well," said I, "has your husband gone?" "No, but he's agwine tomorrow, and I'm getting something for him now." "Don't you feel sorry as the time approaches for him to go?" "Oh, yes, I shall miss him mightily; but I ain't never cried about it; I never shed a tear for the old man, nor for the boys neither, and I ain't agwine to. Them Yankees not come a-nigh to Richmond; if they does I will fight them myself. The women must fight, for they *shan't* cross Mayo's   **page 99/**   Bridge; they *shan't* git to Richmond." I said to her, "You are a patriot." "Yes, honey — ain't you? Ain't everybody?" I was sorry to leave this heroine in home-spun, but she was too busy buying cakes, etc., for the "old man" to be interrupted any longer. **page 100/**

No. 62   The Richmond *Enquirer,* April 25, 1862, p. 1.

Provisions and the Hucksters

It is found by those upon whom it devolves to provide family supplies, that the late schedule of prices fixed upon by the Provost Marshal for the relief of our citizens, has quite a contrary effect. It is complained that while the prices are regulated and diminished, the supply of provisions is curtailed. The great scarcity of provisions is acknowledged by everyone; but it is not to be wondered at when we consider the great increase of our floating population, together with the fact that hucksters refuse to furnish the markets at the established prices. Some other remedy should be sought for this evil.

No. 63   George Cary Eggleston, *A Rebel's Recollections,* New York, G. P. Putnam's Sons, 1905.

The effects of the extreme depreciation of the currency were sometimes almost ludicrous. One of my friends, a Richmond lady, narrowly escaped very serious trouble in an effort to practice a wise economy. Anything for which the dealers did not ask an outrageously high price seemed wonderfully cheap always, and she, at least, lacked the self-control necessary to abstain from buying largely whenever she found anything the price of which was lower than she had supposed it would be. Going into the market one morning with "stimulated ideas of prices," as she phrased it, the consequence of having paid a thousand dollars   **page 100/**   for a barrel of flour, she was surprised to find nearly everything selling for considerably less than she had expected. Thinking that for some unexplained cause there was a temporary depression in prices, she purchased pretty largely in a good many directions, buying, indeed, several things for which she had almost no use at all, and buying considerably more than she needed of other articles. As she was quitting the market on foot, — for it had become disreputable in Richmond to ride in a carriage, and the ladies would not do it on any account — she was tapped on the shoulder by an officer who told her that she was under arrest, for buying in the market to sell again. As the lady was well known to prominent people she was speedily released, but she thereafter curbed her propensity to buy freely of cheap things. Buying to sell again had been forbidden under severe penalties, — an absolutely necessary measure for the protection of the people against the   **page 101/**   rapacity of the hucksters, who, going early into the markets, would buy literally everything there, and by agreement among themselves double or quadruple the already exorbitant rates.   **page 102/**

No. 64   George Cary Eggleston, *A Rebel's Recollections*, New York, G. P. Putnam's Sons, 1905.

. . . the disproportion between the prices of different articles was not greater than that between the cost of goods imported through the blockade and their selling price. The usual custom of blockade-running firms was to build or buy a steamer in Europe, bring it to Nassau in ballast, and load it there with assorted merchandise. Selling this cargo in Charleston or Wilmington for Confederate money, they would buy cotton with which to reload the ship for her outward voyage. The owner of many of these ships once told me that if a vessel which had brought in one cargo were lost with a load of cotton on her outward voyage, the owner would lose nothing, the profits on the merchandise being fully equal to the entire value of ship and cotton. If he could get one cargo of merchandise in, and one of cotton out, the loss of the ship with a second cargo of merchandise would still leave him a clear profit of more than a hundred per cent. upon his investment.   **page 87/**   And this was due solely to the abnormal state of prices in the country, and not at all to the management of the blockade-runners. They sold their cargoes at auction, and bought cotton in the open market.

Their merchandise brought fabulous prices, while cotton, for want of a market, remained disproportionately low. That the merchants engaged in this trade were in no way the authors of the state of prices may be seen from two facts. First, if I am correctly informed, they uniformly gave the government an opportunity to take such articles as it had need of, and especially all the quinine imported, at the price fixed in Richmond, without regard to the fact that speculators would pay greatly more for the goods. In one case within my knowledge a heavy invoice of quinine was sold to the government for eleven hundred dollars an ounce, when a speculator stood ready to take it at double the price. Secondly, the cargo sales were peremptory, and **page 88/** speculators sometimes combined and bought a cargo considerably below the market price, by appearing at the sale in such numbers as to exclude all other **page 89/**   bidders.

No. 65 *Southern Historical Society Papers,* Richmond, Virginia, 1876-1943, vol. XVII (49 vols.).

> *[From the oration of Colonel Charles Marshall, Lee's Military Secretary, at the occasion of the laying of the cornerstone of the Lee Monument in Richmond, October 27, 1887.]*

Richmond, after the destruction of the *Virginia* in April, 1862, became practically a frontier port, but its possession was necessary to prevent the loss of Virginia and the transfer of the war south of the Roanoke. **page 238/**

. . . . . .

Richmond depended for the support of its inhabitants, and the army that defended Richmond depended for its supplies of all kinds, upon long and exposed lines of railway, the defense of which was necessary, if Richmond was to be held.

Now, if you will count the whole number of Federal troops employed for three years in trying to take Richmond, including, of course, those engaged in destroying supplies upon which Richmond and its defenders directly depended, and in breaking lines of rail by which Richmond received its supplies and the army defending Richmond received nearly everything it required, and then count all the troops engaged during that time in defending Richmond and its communications, you will find that the respective numbers were nearly or quite as four to one.

Then, if you remember that the defense of these communications, as well as the defense of the city, was imposed upon the smaller force, and that the larger had the aid of a powerful flotilla, and the assailants had a profusion of military supplies of all kinds, and that the defenders were armed mainly with the spoils of battle, and very often were nearly naked and always had little to eat, and that there were ten men to take the place of every Federal soldier lost, and often none to fill a vacancy in the Confederate ranks, I say, if you remember all these things and then reflect that Richmond was held triumphantly for three years, I think you will understand how it is that the consent of military opinion in our day accords a foremost place among the great soldiers of ancient and modern times to our chieftain of the glancing helm and stainless sword. **page 329/**

No. 66 The Richmond *Enquirer,* May 3, 1862, p.1.

A Growl at the Growlers

The city of Richmond contains many refugees — citizens and families who have left their homes to escape the neighborship or domination of the enemy's forces. Many of these are fresh from their sacrifices of home comforts and property interests. Among the resident citizens, too, there is a considerable feeling of insecurity, and of consequent uneasiness; not only such as is properly due to the designs and the nearness of the enemy and the uncertainties of war, but the anxiety which originates with the nervous and spreads by contagion. There are enough here of men, by courtesy if Lincoln's law for arresting alarmists were in force to crowd Castle Godwin [a prison] before noon of this day; and there are many others who set their countenances by the alarmists' faces, as a man sets his watch by the town clock.

It is natural that men should be excited by recent misfortunes, and by seeming approaching perils. But we should not therefore surrender our fortitude nor renounce our trust. We should not permit ourselves to feel that the country is lost because our individual homes are lost or endangered. We should take a more comprehensive view of things; and such a view, we are persuaded, will not justify those alarms which the men of white lips and blanched cheeks, and startled vision, have made it their business to propogate, and those clamors with which it is so fashionable to assail all in authority, as if they were the conscious authors of the alleged impending ruin.

. . . .

"But we have no confidence in the administration," says one. Why have you not, sir? "They intend to abandon Richmond and Virginia." This, we are perfectly confident, is utterly without any foundation in fact. Virginia's fields, alas, may be ensanguined by the blood of many a hero, but she will not be abandoned. The very falling back of which such querulous complaint is made, was for her better defense and that of her Capital. We are certainly not removed beyond the contingencies of war; but that a bold, brave, gigantic effort will be made to defend us, we are sure; and that Heaven will prosper it with success we confidently believe. . . .

But the President is so obstinate, says another. He will take nobody's suggestions. No quality on earth is more important to one in Mr. Davis' situation than firmness and decision. If he carries these to the extent of obstinancy, and contempt for the opinions of his advisers, it is certainly a fault and a misfortune to the country. But really, we have not seen the proof of it. It surely is not found in his confession that in attempting to defend our whole frontier from invasion he had attempted too much. There are few prominent men whose pride of opinion would not have forbidden so frank a confession — foreseeing, too, the use which his critics would make of it. And it was a mistake made, we dare say, in tenderness to those very wishes of individuals to which he is alleged to be indifferent.

That the President listens with respect to all intelligent suggestions, and gives all the time his duties will allow to such as wish to speak with him, is undoubtedly true. But that he finally forms his own opinion and acts upon it, is equally certain and equally proper. He is earnestly advised to do at one and the same time the most contradictory and the most impossible things, and non-compliance is held as proof of obstinacy! We must learn to be more patient, more just, less censorious, and more helpful. Our affairs are much more cheerful in their present aspect, when viewed aright than the gloomy suppose, and our ultimate triumph is as certain as that the shades of the coming night will be followed by the rising of tomorrow's sun.

No. 67 Official Records of the Union and Confederate Armies, series I, volume XI, part III, Washington, Government Printing Office, 1884.

Engineer Bureau,
Richmond, May 9, 1862.

John B. Stanard,
    In charge of Richmond Defenses:
    Sir: Colonel Goode, Major Allen, and other artillery officers have been directed to mount the 32-pounder guns on ship carriages around this city, and I wish you to point out to these officers, as I have pointed out to you, the places where they are to place the guns, and furnish them every facility for forwarding the work at your command. page 504/

Alfred L. Rives,
Acting Chief Engineer Bureau.

No. 68 Official Records of the Union and Confederate Armies, series I, volume XI, part III, Washington, Government Printing Office, 1902.

War Department, C.S.A.,
Richmond, Va., May 10, 1862.

S. Cooper,
    Adjutant and Inspector General:
    Sir: Have such of your records and papers as ought to be preserved, and are not required for constant reference, packed in boxes, for removal and marked, so as to designate the bureau to which they belong. Books and papers necessary for constant reference may be kept in the presses, but boxes must be prepared for them. This is only intended as a prudent step, and is not caused by any bad news from the army. There is no need, therefore, for any panic in the city, and it should be prevented by the assurance that we have every reason to think that the city can be successfully defended. page 504/

G. W. Randolph,
Secretary of War.

No. 69 The Richmond Enquirer, May 13, 1862, p.1.

Rowdyism

The lower orders of society have grown accustomed to the glitter of bayonets about the streets, and no longer suffer from the dread of being punched through for kicking up a row. The old order of rowdyism is returning, and every night has some free fight or noisy outdoor bacchanal to record. The other night we had a double murder; several almost similar cases had occurred a short time before, and since, the nocturnal sprees of rowdies of all kinds have rendered nights hideous in some quarters of the city. This state of things should not be ignored by the proper authorities. Rowdyism should be put down and kept down.

No. 70   Judith W. McGuire, *Diary of a Southern Refugee,* New York, E. J. Hale & Son, 1867.

May 14, 1862: The anxiety of all classes for the safety of   **page 112/**   Richmond is now intense, though a strong faith in the goodness of God and the valour of our troops keeps us calm and hopeful. A gentleman, high in position, panic-struck, was heard to exclaim, yesterday: "Norfolk has fallen, Richmond will fall, Virginia is to be given up, and tomorrow I shall leave this city [Richmond] an exile and a beggar." Others are equally despondent, and, as is too frequently the case in times of trouble, attribute all our disasters to the incompetency and faithlessness of those entrusted with the administration of public affairs. Even General Lee does not escape animadversion, and the President is the subject of the most bitter maledictions. I have been shocked to hear that a counter-revolution, if not openly advocated, has been distinctly foreshadowed, as the only remedy for our ills. The public authorities of Richmond, greatly moved by the defenceless condition of the city, appointed a committee, and appropriated funds to aid in completing the obstructions at Drury's [sic] Bluff. . . .   **page 113/**

No. 71   John B. Jones, *A Rebel War Clerk's Diary,* New York, Old Hickory Bookshop, 1935, vol. I (2 vols.).

May 19, 1862: We await the issue before Richmond. It is still believed by many that it is the intention of the government and the generals to evacuate the city. . . . Wrote as strong a letter as I could to the President, stating what I have every reason to believe would be the consequences of the abandonment of Richmond. There would be demoralization and even insubordination in the army. Better die here! With the exception of the business portion of the city, the enemy could not destroy a great many homes by bombardment. But if defeated and driven back, our troops would make a heroic defense in the streets, in the walled grave-yards, and from the windows. Better electrify the world by such scenes of heroism, than surrender the capital and endanger the cause. I besought him by every consideration, not to abandon Richmond to the enemy short of the last extremity.

    The legislature has also passed resolutions calling upon the C. S. Government to defend Richmond at all hazards, relieving the Confederate authorities, in advance, of all responsibility for any damage sustained.   **page 126/**

No. 72 Constance Cary Harrison, *Recollections, Grave and Gay,* New York, Charles Scribner's Sons, 1912.

We had come to the end of May [1862], when the eyes of the whole continent turned toward Richmond. On the 31st Johnston assaulted the Federals, who had advanced to Seven Pines! It was so near that the first guns sent our hearts into our mouths, like a sudden loud knocking at one's door at night. The women left in Richmond had, with few exceptions, husbands, fathers, sons and brothers in the fight. I have never seen a finer exhibition of calm courage than they showed in this baptism of fire. No one wept or moaned aloud. All went about their task of preparing for the wounded, making bandages, scraping lint, improvising beds. Night brought a lull in the frightful cannonading. We threw ourselves dressed upon our beds to get a little rest before the morrow.

During the night began the ghastly procession of wounded brought in from the field. Every vehicle the city could produce supplemented the military ambulances. Many slightly wounded men, so black with gunpowder as to be unrecognizable, came limping in on foot. All next day, women with white faces flitted bareheaded through the streets and hospitals, looking for their own. Churches and lecture-rooms were thrown open for volunteer ladies sewing and filling the rough beds called for by the surgeons. There was not enough of *anything* to meet the sudden appalling call of many strong men stricken unto death. Hearing that my cousin, Reginald Hyde, was reported wounded, two of us girls volunteered to help his mother to search for him through the lower hospitals. We tramped down Main Street through the hot sun over burning pavements, **page 82/** from one scene of horror to another, bringing up finally at the St. Charles Hotel, a large old building. What a sight met our eyes! Men in every stage of mutilation, lying waiting for the surgeons upon bare boards, with haversacks or army blankets, or nothing, beneath their heads. Some gave up the weary ghost as we passed them by. All were suffering keenly and needed ordinary attention. To be there empty-handed nearly broke our hearts. Bending down over bandaged faces stiff with blood and thick with flies, nothing did we see or hear of the object of our search, who, I am glad to say, arrived later at his mother's house, to be nursed by her to a speedy recovery.

The impression of that day was ineffaceable. It left me permanently convinced that nothing is worth war!

. . . Gradually, some order came out of the chaos of overtasked hospital service. The churches gave their seat cushions to make beds; the famous old wine cellars of private houses sent their priceless Madeira, port, sherry, and brandy; everybody's cook was set to turning out dainties, and for our own men we begged unblushingly until they were fairly well supplied. At night, carrying palm-leaf fans, we sauntered out into the streets scarcely less hot than in full sunshine. Once, literally panting for a fresh **page 83/** breath of air, a party of us went with an official of the Capitol up through the vapor bath of many steep stairs, to emerge on a little platform on the summit of the building. There — oh! joy — were actually breezes that brought relief. There we sat and looked down on the city that could not sleep, and talked, or listened to the voice of the river, that I seemed to hear yet over the tramp of rusty battalions, the short imperious stroke of the alarm bell, the clash of passing bands, the gallop of horsemen, the roar of battle, the moan of hospitals, the stifled note of sorrow — all the Richmond war sounds, sacred and unforgettable.

Day after day one heard the wailing dirge of military bands preceding a soldier's funeral. One could not number those sad pageants in our leafy streets; the coffin with its cap and sword and gloves, the riderless horse with empty boots in the stirrups of an army saddle! Such soldiers as could be spared from the front marching with arms reversed and crape-shrouded banners, passers-by standing with bare bent heads. page 84/

No. 73   The Richmond *Enquirer*, May 31, 1862, p.1.

The City

A few days have flitted rapidly by, and Richmond, the noisy, crowded and motley, has subsided into a semblance of its former self. — Between the calls to duty and the lampoons of the newspapers, the streets have been divested of their blue and gold embellishments, straggling soldiers, to a great extent, have disappeared, and flashing steeds on pleasure bent have resigned their fine clad jockeys to the fate of [word indistinguishable, probably war].

Many private families have been removed to more genial and less accessible localities, in view of the possibilities of danger, and several seminaries have suspended their sessions until the storm is past and the victory won. There has been no helter-skelter running away, no silly excitement, no tearful forebodings of evil. The number of temporary absentees is comparatively very small, and is confined exclusively to the more delicate portion of the gentler sex.

The streets are still beautiful with the presence of ladies, and it would be difficult exceedingly to detect any alteration in the general appearance of the city, so far as they are concerned.

No. 74   Mrs. G. E. Pickett, *Pickett and His Men*, Philadelphia, J. B. Lippincott Company, 1913.

The battle [Seven Pines] brought the war closer to me than any other had yet done. The school had closed and my vacation was just beginning. I could not return to my home, which was within Federal lines, and my mother had accepted an invitation for me from friends in Richmond.

The library and parlors of the beautiful home of my friends had been given up for the comfort of the wounded soldiers. The city was in tears; the horrors of war had become a reality. Busy, bustling, sad enough scenes were being enacted on every side. New regiments from the far South had but just arrived and were marching through the streets, cheering and waving their hats as they passed. Batteries of artillery were hurrying along the thoroughfares, all going toward the front, down Main and Broad streets into the Williamsburg road. Long lines of ambulances coming from the opposite way toiled slowly along, filled with the wounded from the battle-field who were being carried to the various hospitals, the long, torturing way marked by the trail of blood that oozed drop by drop from human veins. Here and there might be seen a wagon-load of dead, piled one upon another, their stiffened, rigid feet exposed to view, showing to the horrified spectators that for just so many the cares and   page 82/   sorrows of this life, its pains and miseries, were passed forever. Every vehicle of any description was utilized and crowded to its utmost capacity. The less severely wounded were made to walk, and long lines of them could be seen hobbling along the streets, their wounds bound up in bloody rags.

The citizens turned out in full force and did all in their power to alleviate the sufferings of the soldiers. Not a home in all the city wherein some wounded were not taken to be nursed with tenderest care. Every possible space, parlors, passages, and chambers, were converted into temporary hospitals, and everything done that unwearied nursing and gentlest attention could devise, and that for the roughest soldier in the ranks as readily as for the general who wore the stars. Women stood before their doors with wine and food, ministering it unsparingly to the wounded going by.

The Capitol Square, the news-mart and general rendezvous at all times for the soldiers, was now filled with officers, privates, and citizens, and many who were in doubt as to the fate of some loved one, turned their steps to this little park as the surest and easiest way of gaining information. Comrades met and congratulated each other on escape. Citizens were listening to recitals of the battle. Dirty, mud-covered soldiers, husbands, brothers and lovers, were clasped in whitest arms.

The soft-voiced women of the South had dauntless souls, and when sobbing in agony at parting they yet could murmur with pallid lips like the Spartan mother when handing the shield to her son — "Return with it or upon it!"

It had been a terrible day of anxiety to the people of Richmond. All day long the cannon had thundered and roared. With agonized feelings they had listened to the page 83/   death-sounds, and with nerves strained to the highest tension awaited the results. Not only did they have their own near and dear to think of, but from all the South had poured in letters to friends and relatives, with the sacred charge, "care for and watch out for our loved ones if wounded." From all quarters of the Confederacy wives followed their husbands to the scene of action. Every available house, public and private, was sought for by the refugees in the city.

To these strangers in a strange land it had been a trial of no slight moment to listen to those death-dealing monsters and know that a dear one's life was at stake.

Ah, yes; this battle had thrilled the city to its center. Richmond authorities were unprepared for so extraordinary a call upon their accommodations. Buildings were hastily fitted up with the barest of comforts; medical and all other stores were inadequate to the demand. The doctors were employed day and night. The women, young and old, volunteered their services as nurses. In every house soups and other delicacies were made for the wounded. Though much suffering was in a degree mitigated, many a precious life, which otherwise might have been saved, was lost for want of ordinary attention.

For days and nights wagons and ambulances never ceased to empty their wretched loads before the doors of each of these hastily improvised hospitals until the buildings overflowed with maimed humanity. There was not an empty store in which rude pallets were not strewn over the floor and counter. In the dressing of the wounds — rough it must have seemed, in spite of every effort to make it gentle — the racking of quivering nerves passed all bounds of patient endurance. Screams of agony would sometimes break out upon the open air with startling emphasis. **page 84/**

.   .   .   .

So the long procession of wounded, nearly five thousand, young boys, middle-aged and white-haired men, from the private to the highest ranks, hurt in every conceivable manner, suffering in every way; parched, feverish, agonized, wearing a look of mute agony no words may describe, or else lapsed into a fortunate unconsciousness, wended their way to the hospitals.

There went men from every State, pouring out blood like water and offering up lives of sacrifice for the cause they had espoused. No city in all the world was sadder than our Richmond in those days. All the miseries and woes of Seven Pines had been emptied into her fair homes and streets. She had "no language but a cry," an exceedingly bitter cry, that rose in its might to God on high "if the heavens were not brass."

As you walked the streets some scene to make the heart ache would be enacted before your eyes. The dreaded ambulance might draw up before some residence whose doors would open to receive a burden borne in tenderly, brother, son, or husband. There would gather hastily on the steps members of the family to receive him, dead or hurt. **page 85/**

From some wife, sister, or mother you heard words of tenderest meaning, or bitterest weeping, or scream of agony as you passed along; or it might be that you caught only a look of mute despair as if she had turned to stone, for we take such things differently, we women.

Black waved its sad signal from door to door. It was no unusual thing to see four or five funeral possessions at the same time on their way to the city of the dead.

People realized with a sudden shock the actualities of an internecine strife; it was brought to their very doors. Before they had seen only its pride and pomp, and its martial showing. They had heard only the rattling of artillery over the stony streets, and the tread of passing columns. All at once, with the sound of hostile guns, gaunt, grim-visaged war touched their hearts and sickened their souls with horror.

It rendered them more determined, more earnest, more sincere. It made them feel that it was a time to perform their part of the great tragedy, and not waste the hours in light comedy, vain regrets, or childish longings. In one day Richmond was changed from a mirth-loving, pleasure-seeking place, into a city of resolute men and women, nerved to make any sacrifice for their cause. **page 86/**

No. 75 *Southern Historical Society Papers,* Richmond, Virginia, 1876-1943, vol. XXXVI (49 vols.).

[Abstract from an address of Dr. J. R. Gildersleeve, president of the Association of Medical Officers of the Army and Navy of the Confederacy, at Nashville, Tenn., June 14, 1904. From the News Leader, Richmond, Va., *January 7, 1909.]*

History of Chimborazo Hospital, C.S.A.

East of the city of Richmond, whilom capital of the Confederate States, and separated from the city proper by the historic Bloody Run Creek, is an elevated plateau of nearly forty acres, commanding from its height a grand view. . . .

On this high and picturesque point, so well adapted to hospital purposes, in the year 1862, when the Federal troops moved in force on Bull Run, and the real campaign began, General Joseph E. Johnston reported that nine thousand men would **page 86/** have to be sent back to Richmond for admittance to hospitals before his army could proceed.

. . . .

The surgeon-general had only twenty-five hundred beds when General Johnston made his report. Work was at once commenced, and one hundred and fifty well-constructed and ventilated buildings were erected, each one-hundred feet in length, thirty feet in width, and one story high, though not all built at one time, but as needed to furnish comfortable quarters for the sick and wounded. Five large hospitals or divisions were organized, thirty wards to each division. . . . The hospitals presented the appearance of a large town, imposing and attractive, with its alignment of buildings kept whitened with lime, streets and alleys clean, and with its situation on such an elevated point it commanded a grand, magnificent, and pleasant view of the surrounding country for many miles.

The divisions of this immense hospital were five, or five hospitals in one, and five surgeons, each one of the five in charge of a division; also a number of assistants and acting assistant surgeons (forty-five to fifty), each in charge of several wards or buildings, and subject to surgeons in divisions, and all subject to Surgeon James B. McCaw, in charge of executive heads.

With natural drainage, the best conceivable on the east, south, and west; good water supply; five large ice houses; Russian bath house; cleanliness and excellent system of removal of wastes, the best treatment, comforts and results in a military hospital in times of war were secured. **page 87/**

. . . .

The hospital never drew fifty dollars from the Confederate States government, but relied solely upon the money received from commutation of rations. The medical departments and subsistence departments were organized all to themselves, and the money from commuted rations was used to buy what was necessary.

The hospital trading canal boat, "Chimborazo," Lawrence Lottier in command, plied between Richmond, Lynchburg and Lexington, bartering cotton, yarn, shoes, etc., for provisions. This was only one of the hospital's many resources. **page 89/**

.   .   .   .

The total number of patients received and treated at Chimborazo Hospital amounted to seventy-six thousand (out of this number about 17,000 were wounded soldiers), and it was the first military hospital in point of size in this country and in the world. . . . The percentage of **page 90/** deaths at Chimborazo was a fraction over nine per cent. Complete records were kept, and are still in existence in the office of the surgeon-general at Washington, D.C. . . . **page 91/**

No. 76   The Richmond *Enquirer,* June 18, 1862, p. 1.

A Brief Address from General Stuart

On Monday afternoon, during a drill of the Richmond Battalion, General J. E. B. Stuart appeared on the Capitol Square, and upon being recognized, the enthusiasm which followed was tremendous. The air was vocal for a time with "Hurrahs for Stuart" and the people, citizens and soldiers, were pretty near crazy to hear the gallant General speak. Appeals were made to him from two hundred tongues to address the assembly. At length, the General assented, and ascending the steps of the Governor's Mansion, bowed gracefully and modestly to the crowd, and returned them his heart-felt acknowledgments; and paying a brief tribute to the spirit of the people, the grand object of Southern deliverance, and the determined and heroic character of our army, descended amidst the ring of deafening cheers.

No. 77   Heros von Borcke, *Memoirs of the Confederate War for Independence,* Edinburgh and London, William Blackwood and Sons, 1866, vol. I (2 vols.).

The Spotswood Hotel at this time [early July, 1862] was crowded with guests, among whom a neighbour of my own, was no less distinguished a person than a Federal General, M'Call, who had been taken prisoner in one of the recent battles. As might naturally have been expected, the joy of the people of Richmond was very great at the deliverance of their city from the hands of the enemy; but they took their good fortune with a very becoming composure, and spoke and acted just as if, in their judgment, with such an army as that of General Lee, under such commanders, between them and the invading force, the struggle for the Confederate capital could have had no other result. No powder was wasted in salutes over the victory, no bonfires blazed, no windows were illuminated, and the general appearance of Richmond was in all respects unchanged from what it had been a month before. **page 75/**

No. 78   *The Southern Literary Messenger,* Richmond, July and August, 1862, p. 503.

Editor's Table

Of all *nil admirai,* the people of Richmond must be accounted the foremost. Nothing excites them — they exhibit no emotion. When 100,000 foes besieged the city; they went about their business as usual. When the battle, which was to decide the fate of the Confederate capital, perhaps of the Confederacy itself, began they took it very coolly, — and went on about their business. They said, "Jackson's come, and we know how it is going to end." The thunder of battle seemed to excite some of the girls like champagne — that was the only manifestation. When the victory was achieved, there was no Yankee-Chinese hullabulloo, no loud jubilation, no ringing of bells, no firing of cannon, standing on the head or kicking of the heels in the air. Many and great victories have been vouchsafed the Confederate arms, but the only guns fired in Richmond were on the occasion of the fall of Fort Sumter. Since then, both good and evil fortune have been received with equanimity almost stolidity.

Nor do the people of Richmond go into ecstacies over victorious generals. Magruder came, after Bethel, and there was no demonstration. Price came, and all was quiet. Johnston arrived, and there was not even a serenade. The President rides or walks the streets, and nobody turns a head. Even Lee is regarded by the citizens of Richmond as any other man.

Soldiers came crowding from all parts of the Confederacy to the defense of Richmond. The people did not so much as cheer them as they marched in column down the Main Street to the field of battle. But when they came back wounded, they turned out *en masse* to feed and nurse them.

The people of Richmond are certainly remarkable people. . . .

No. 79   Constance Cary Harrison, *Recollections, Grave and Gay,* New York, Charles Scribner's Sons, 1912.

. . . Except for the numbers of people swathed in black met in the thoroughfares, Richmond showed little trace of its battle summer. As yet the pinch of the times did not greatly affect the home commissariat, although we refugees had to be satisfied with simple living in other people's rooms, since a whole house to ourselves simply could not be thought of. When asked into private houses we found tables laid, as of old, with shining silver and porcelain and snowy damask, although the bill of fare was unpretending. The custom of giving the best of everything to the hospitals went on till the end of the war. Society was reinforced by a number of agreeable and high-bred women from all parts of the South, many of whom had previously graced a wider social sphere in Europe and America. Its peculiar attraction lay in the total absence of pretence. People thus bound by a common tie of interest and poignant sympathy tolerated no assumption of superior fashion in any of their number. In such an atmosphere flourishes best the old-fashioned grace of neighborliness. To the very last, each refugee family shared what it had with the other; while Richmond folk threw open their broad, delightful homes to receive their friends, with or without gastronomic entertainment; lent furniture to those in need, and sent dainty little dishes to the sick. All rejoiced in each other's joys, grieved with each other's griefs. Hardships in such company were lightened   **page 94/** of their weight. Sorrows so shared were easier to bear.   **page 95/**

No. 80   Catherine C. Hopley, *Life in the South,* London, Chapman and Hall, 1863, vol. II (2 vols.).

I had found no soap in my apartment, and told the chambermaid there was none.
"Soap!"
"Yes."
"No, nor hasn't been dis yeah long time."
"What do people do for soap then?"
"Why folks jes goes out an' gits it to suit theirselves, jes whar ever they can fine any."
A very doubtful "suit" that, one would fancy. I passed a very pretty little child, in its nurse's arms, on the stairs. I asked its name.
"Jeffersonia."
The last child's name I had asked was "Beauregard," a little negro baby. Another was "General Lee." There will be no want of "Generals" in the Confederacy for at least a generation to come, so far as names are concerned.   **page 357/**

No. 81   Mary Boykin Chesnut, *A Diary from Dixie,* Boston, Houghton Mifflin Company, 1949.

1862: Turkeys were thirty dollars apiece, but Lawrence [servant] kept us plentifully supplied and Molly [cook] cooked admirably. We lived well, kept open house, indeed. Our friends the soldiers from the army breakfasted, dined, and supped at the corner of Clay and Twelfth Streets. We had sent us from home wine, rice, potatoes, hams, eggs, butter and pickles about once a month. A man came on with all that the plantation could furnish us.   **page 283/**

No. 82   The Southern Illustrated News, September 13, 1862, p. 8.

. . . the Drama in our city at the present time is, we are sorry to say, at a decidedly low ebb. The legitimate Drama has been laid on the shelf, and we fear there it will remain, until dramatic talent enough is procured to raise it from its resting place, and brush off the cobwebs and dust, which from the quiescent life it has led for some time, are becoming as thick as the "fuzz on an antiquated apple pie. . . ."

No. 83   George Cary Eggleston, *A Rebel's Recollections,* New York, G. P. Putnam's Sons, 1905.

I can hardly hope to make the ex-soldier of the Union understand fully how we on the other side were fed in the field. He fought and marched with a skilled commissariat at his back, and, for his further staff of comfort, had the Christian and Sanitary Commissions, whose handy tin cups and other camp conveniences came to us only through the uncertain and irregular channel of abandonment and capture; and unless his imagination be a vivid one, he will not easily conceive the state of our commissariat or the privations we suffered as a consequence of its singularly bad management. The first trouble was, that we had   **page 200/**   for a commissary-general a crotchety doctor, some of whose acquaintances had for years believed him insane. Aside from his suspected aberration, and the crotchets which had made his life already a failure, he knew nothing whatever of the business belonging to the department under his control, his whole military experience having consisted of a few years' service as a lieutenant of cavalry in one of the Territories, many years before the date of his appointment as chief of subsistence in the Confederacy. Wholly without experience to guide him, he was forced to evolve from his own badly balanced intellect whatever system he could adopt, and from the beginning of the war until the early part of the year 1865, the Confederate armies were forced to lean upon this broken reed in the all-important matter of food supply. The generals commanding in the field, we are told on the very highest authority, protested, suggested, remonstrated almost   **page 201/**   daily, but their remonstrances were unheeded and their suggestions set at naught. At Manassas, where the army was well-nigh starved out in the very beginning of the war, food might have been abundant but for the obstinacy of this one man. On our left lay a country unsurpassed, and almost unequaled in productiveness. It was rich in grain and meat, these being its special products. A railroad, with next to nothing to do, penetrated it, and its stores of food were nearly certain to be exposed to the enemy before any other part of the country should be conquered. The obvious duty of the commissary-general, therefore, was to draw upon that section for the supplies which were both convenient and abundant. The chief of subsistence ruled otherwise, however, thinking it better to let that source of supply lie exposed to the first advance of the enemy, while we drew upon the Richmond *dépôts* for a daily ration, and shipped it by the overtasked   **page 202/**   line of railway leading from the capital to Manassas. It was nothing to him that he was thus exhausting the rear and crippling the resources of the country for the future. It was nothing to him that in the midst of plenty the army was upon a short allowance of food. It was nothing that the shipments of provisions from Richmond by this railroad seriously interfered with other important interests. System was everything, and this was a part of his system. The worst of it was, that in this all-important branch of the service experience and organization wrought little if any improvement as the war went on, so that as the supplies and the means of transportation grew smaller, the undiminished inefficiency of the department produced disastrous results. The army, suffering for food, was disheartened by the thought that the scarcity was due to the exhaustion of the country's resources. Red tape was supreme, and no sword was permitted to cut it. I   **page 203/**   remember one little circumstance, which will serve to illustrate the absoluteness with which system was suffered to override sense in the administration of the affairs of the subsistence department. I served for a time on the coast of South Carolina, a country which produces rice in great abundance, and in which fresh pork and mutton might then be had almost for the asking, while the climate is wholly unsuited to the making of flour or bacon. Just at that time, however, the officials of the commissary department saw fit to feed the whole army on bacon and flour, articles which, if given to troops in that quarter of the country at all, must be brought several hundred miles by rail. The local commissary officers made vigorous suggestions looking to the use of the provisions of which the country round about was full, but, so far as I could learn, no attention whatever was paid to them. At the request of one of these post commmissaries, I wrote an **page 204/**   elaborate and respectful letter on the subject, setting forth the fact that rice, sweet potatoes, corn meal, hominy, grits, mutton, and pork existed in great abundance in the immediate neighborhood of the troops, and could be bought for less than one third the cost of the flour and bacon we were eating. The letter was signed by the post commissary, and forwarded through the regular channels, with the most favorable indorsements possible, but it resulted in nothing. The department presently found it impossible to give us full rations of bacon and flour, but it still refused to think of the remedy suggested. It cut down the ration instead, thus reducing the men to a state of semi-starvation in a country full of food. Relief came at last in the shape of a technicality, else it would not have been allowed to come at all. A vigilant captain discovered that the men were entitled by law to commutation in money for rations, at fixed rates, and acting upon this the men   **page 205/**   were able to buy, with the money paid them in lieu of rations, an abundance of fresh meats and vegetables; and most of the companies managed at the same time to save a considerable fund for future use out of the surplus, so great was the disparity between the cost of the food they bought and that which the government wished to furnish them.

The indirect effect of all this stupidity — for it can be called by no softer name — was almost as bad as its direct results. The people at home, finding that the men in the field were suffering for food, undertook to assist in supplying them. With characteristic profusion they packed boxes and sent them to their soldier friends and acquaintances, particularly during the first year of the war. Sometimes these supplies were permitted to reach their destination, and sometimes they were allowed to decay in a depot because of some failure on the part of the sender to comply with the mysterious page 206/ canons of official etiquette. In either case they were wasted. If they got to the army; they were used wastefully by the men, who could not carry them and had no place of storage for them. If they were detained anywhere, they remained there until some change of front made it necessary to destroy them. There seemed to be nobody invested with sufficient authority to turn them to practical account. I remember a box of my own, packed with cooked meats, vegetable, fruits, — all perishable, — which got within three miles of my tent, but could get no farther, although I hired a farmer's wagon with which to bring it to camp, where my company was at that moment in sore need of its contents. There was some informality, — the officer having it in charge could not tell me what, — about the box itself, or its transmission, or its arrival, or something else, and so it could not be delivered to me, though I had the warrant of my colonel in writing, for page 207/ receiving it. Dismissing my wagoner, I told the officer in charge that the contents of the box were of a perishable character, and that rather than have them wasted, I should be glad to have him accept the whole as a present to his mess; but he declined, on the ground that to accept the present would be a gross irregularity so long as there was an embargo upon the package. I received the box three months later, after its contents had become entirely worthless. Now this is but one of a hundred cases within my own knowledge, and it will serve to show the reader how the inefficiency of the subsistence department led to a wasteful expenditure of those private stores of food which constituted our only reserve for the future. page 208/

. . . .

But it was in Richmond that routine was carried to its absurdest extremities. There, everything was done by rule except those things to which system of some sort would have been of advantage, and they were left at loose ends. Among other page 209/   things a provost system was devised and brought to perfection during the time of martial law. Having once tasted the sweets of despotic rule, its chief refused to resign any part of his absolute sovereignty over the city, even when the reign of martial law ceased by limitation of time. His system of guards and passports was a very marvel of annoying inefficiency. It effectually blocked the way of every man who was intent upon doing his duty, while it gave unconscious but sure protection to spies, blockade-runners, deserters, and absentees without leave from the armies. It was omnipotent for the annoyance of soldier and citizen, but utterly worthless for any good purpose. If a soldier on furlough or even on detached duty arrived in Richmond, he was taken in charge by the provost guards at the railway station, marched to the soldier's home or some other vile prison house, and kept there in durance during the whole time of his stay. It mattered page 210/ not how legitimate his papers were, or how evident his correctness of purpose. The system required that he should be locked up, and locked up he was, in every case, until one plucky fellow made fight by appeal to the courts, and so compelled the abandonment of a practice for which there was never any warrant in law or necessity in fact.

Richmond being the railroad center from which the various lines radiated, nearly every furloughed soldier and officer on leave was obliged to pass through the city, going home and returning. Now to any ordinary intelligence it would seem that a man bearing a full description of himself, and a furlough signed by his captain, colonel, brigadier, division commander, lieutenant-general, and finally by Robert E. Lee as general-in-chief, might have been allowed to go peaceably to his home by the nearest route. But that was no ordinary intelligence which ruled Richmond. Its ability to find places in which to interfere was unlimited, and it decreed that no   **page 211/** soldier should leave Richmond, either to go home or to return direct to the army, without a brown paper passport, signed by an officer appointed for that purpose, and countersigned by certain other persons whose authority to sign or countersign anything nobody was ever able to trace to its source. If any such precaution had been necessary, it would not have been so bad, or even being unnecessary, if there had been the slightest disposition on the part of those passport people to facilitate obedience to their own requirements, the long-suffering officers and men of the army would have uttered no word of complaint. But the facts were exactly the reverse. The passport officials rigidly maintained the integrity of their office hours, and neither entreaty nor persuasion would induce them in any case to anticipate by a single minute the hour for beginning, or to postpone   **page 212/**   the time of ending their daily duties. I stood one day in their office in a crowd of fellow soldiers and officers, some on furlough going home, some returning after a brief visit, and still others, like myself, going from one place to another under orders and on duty. The two trains by which most of us had to go were both to leave within an hour, and if we should lose them we must remain twenty-four hours longer in Richmond, where the hotel rate was then sixty dollars a day. In full view of these facts, the passport men, daintily dressed, sat there behind their railing, chatting and laughing for a full hour, suffering both trains to depart and all these men to be left over rather than do thirty minutes' work in advance of the improperly fixed office hour. It resulted from this system that many men on three or five days' leave lost nearly the whole of it in delays, going and returning. Many others were kept in Richmond for want of a passport   **page 213/**   until their furloughs expired, when they were arrested for absence without leave, kept three or four days in the guardhouse, and then taken as prisoners to their commands, to which they had tried hard to go of their own motion at the proper time. Finally the abuse became so outrageous that General Lee, in his capacity of general-in-chief, issued a peremptory order forbidding anybody to interfere in any way with officers and soldiers traveling under his written authority. **page 214/**

No. 84   Heros von Borcke, *Memoirs of the Confederate War for Independence,* Edinburgh and London, William Blackwood and Sons, 1866, vol. II (2 vols.).

The counties of Loudoun and Fauquier had known but little as yet [October, 1862] of the devastations of the war, and abounded in supplies of every description, which were eagerly offered for sale by the farmers at moderate prices, and might have subsisted our army for six months. Instead of being permitted to profit by this plenty, we had been compelled for the past two months, through the mismanagement and want of experience of the officials of the Quartermaster's Department at Richmond, and against the earnest   page 6/   remonstrances of General Lee, to draw all our supplies from the capital, whence they were sent by rail to Staunton, there to be packed into waggons [sic] and deported beyond Winchester, a distance of more than one hundred miles after leaving the railroad. The subsistence which was so near at hand was thus left for the enemy, by whom it was afterwards used to the greatest advantage. The importance, nay the necessity, in a war of such magnitude, carried on over so vast and thinly-populated a territory, of establishing great magazines for the collection and storage of provisions for the army, very often occurred to me during the struggle in America, and I have, on several occasions, expressed my opinion with regard to it. Had the Confederate authorities, following Napoleon's example, established at the beginning of the war (when it might easily have been done) large depots of army-supplies at points not exposed, like Richmond, to raids of cavalry, I am convinced that it would have had a material influence on the final issue of the great conflict. The difficulties that were experienced during the last two years of the war in supporting the army, and the terrible privations to which men and animals were subjected in consequence of early maladministration and neglect, can be known only to those who were eyewitnesses of the misfortune and participants in the suffering.   page 7/

No. 85   Varina Howell Davis, *Jefferson Davis*, New York, Belford Company, 1890, vol. II (2 vols.).

The paramount questions of the hour [fall of 1862] were, of course, to arm men for the contest, to procure ships and equip them for the destruction of the merchant marine of the United States, and to form an effective financial policy. On this last point there were many   page 159/   opinions, and there had been many efforts made by members of both houses to convince the Presidency of the expediency of selling cotton to the enemy; a larger party advocated the exportation of all the cotton grown in the country to England. Where the ships were to come from for this immense exportation they did not point out; carriers would not be swift enough to run the blockade, and the cotton would be captured, and serve to supply the manufacturers of New England. The men whose families were in need, and at whose gin-houses the means of relief lay piled in bulky plenty, of course leaned toward the malcontents. When all this cumbrous and unavailable wealth was burned by the Government, the dissatisfaction of some gave tongue. The President and his advisers looked to the stringency of the English cotton market, and the suspension of the manufactories, to send up a ground-swell from the English operatives that would compel recognition, and grudged every pound of cotton exported. Now for the first time there appeared to be an organized party in opposition to the Administration. This might have been weakened by daily social intercourse, and habituated as we were to giving numerous entertainments of an official character, we should gladly have kept up the custom; but during every entertainment,   page 160/   without exception, either the death

of a relation was announced to a guest, or a disaster to the Confederacy was tele-
graphed to the President. He was a nervous dyspeptic by habit, and if he was
forced to eat under any excitement, was ill after it for days. He said he could do
either one duty or the other — give entertainments or administer the Government
— and he fancied he was expected to perform the latter service in preference; and
so we ceased to entertain, except at formal receptions or informal dinners and break-
fasts given to as many as Mr. Davis's health permitted us to invite. In the evening
he was too exhausted to receive informal visitors. The *Examiner* sent forth a wail
of regret over the "parsimony of the Administration." It touched feelingly upon
the deprivation to the young people of Richmond of not being received in the
evening, the assumption of "superior dignity by the satraps," etc. This became a
fierce growl, as it contemplated the awful contingency of the "President getting rich
on his savings."

It would have been much better if the President could have met the Congress,
and the State officials as well as the citizens, socially and often, for the magnetism of
his personality would have greatly mollified their resentments; but for years his
physician had   page 161/   forbidden him to go at all into society in Washington,
and he found this disability greater in Richmond, proportionately to the burden
he bore.

One or two of the generals had their little cliques who sympathized with them.
Some disappointed politicians felt that they had been overlooked, or their claims
disregarded. Some thought they knew that their names had been preferred for the
office which had been conferred upon Mr. Davis; others felt sure that everyone
except the President had preferred them for the portfolios unworthily held by
others. In fact, it was the "Spectator's" allegory of the man who, dissatisfied with his
short face, was allowed to lay it down, and yet could find none other to suit him.
To these malcontents, always noncombatants, the blighter's hand was the President's.

Congressional committees made earnest and honest recommendations to him to
do this or that, ignorant of what had transpired since they formulated their projects
— which were perhaps well conceived when formed, but had become impracticable
from the change of circumstances; a politician would have flattered and appeared to
confide in them without communicating anything, but Mr. Davis was too sincere
for this policy. To have explained   page 162/   these difficulties would often have
exposed the army or navy to danger; he therefore had to take refuge in silence; this
was interpreted to mean contempt or a stubborn desire to dictate to the co-ordinate
branch of government, and increased the discontent.

He was abnormally sensitive to disapprobation: even a child's disapproval dis-
composed him. He felt how much he was misunderstood, and the sense of mortifica-
tion and injustice gave him a repellent manner. It was because of his supersensitive
temperament and the acute suffering it caused him to be misunderstood, I had
deprecated his assuming the civil administration.

He was always inclined to sacrifice himself rather than betray the trust even
of an enemy. Once, when an officer he loved had been censured by one of the
generals in a letter marked "private," and was indicated as one whose removal was
required, the officer remonstrated warmly with the President, and, with the freedom
of old friendship, said, "You know me, how could I ever hold my head up under

implied censure, from you, my old friend?" The President, who could not explain that he found no fault in him, to cover his discomposure said, curtly, "You have, I believe, received your orders; I can suggest nothing but obedience." **page 163/**

His old friend left him wounded to the quick, and Mr. Davis came home and went without eating, to his room and slept little. As soon as he could speak quietly of it, he said: "I would not secretly censure a man and ask another to take the responsibility, but, as the letter was confidential, all I could do was to make the poor fellow too mad with me to ask an explanation." So, little by little, the Congress became alienated, or at least a large portion of them with a few of the military men. The President let the conviction gnaw at his vitals in silence. He used to say with a sigh, "If we succeeed, we shall hear nothing of these malcontents; if we do not, then I shall be held accountable by the majority of friends as well as foes. I will do my best, and God will give me strength to bear whatever comes to me." **page 164/**

No. 86 Judith W. McGuire, *Diary of a Southern Refugee,* New York, E. J. Hale & Son, 1867.

November 29, 1862: . . . The people of Fredericksburg suffer greatly from the sudden move. I know a family, accustomed to every luxury at home, now in a damp basement-room in Richmond. The mother and three young daughters cooking, washing, etc.; the father, a merchant, is sick and cut off from business, friends, and everything else. Another family, consisting of mother and four daughters, in one room, supported by the **page 172/** work of one of the daughters who has an office in the Note-Signing Department. To keep starvation from the house is all that they can do; their supplies in Fredericksburg cannot be brought to them — no transportation. I cannot mention the numbers who are similarly situated; the country is filled with them. . . . How everybody is to be supported is a difficult question to decide. Luxuries have been given up long ago, by many persons. Coffee is $4.00 per pound, and good tea from $18.00 to $20.00; butter ranges from $1.50 to $2 per pound; lard 50 cents; corn $15.00 per barrel; and wheat $4.50 per bushel. We can't get a muslin dress for less than $6 or $8 per yard; calico $1.75, etc. This last is no great hardship, for we will all resort to homespun. We are knitting our own stockings, and regret that we did not learn to spin and weave. The North Carolina homespun is exceedingly pretty, and makes a genteel dress; the only difficulty is in the dye; the colours are pretty, but we have not learned the art of *setting* the wood colours; but we are improving in that art too, and when the first dye fades, we can dip them again in the dye. **page 173/**

No. 87   Mary Boykin Chesnut, *A Diary from Dixie,* Boston, Houghton Mifflin Company, 1949.

1862: [The chronology has broken down here] When I first went back to Richmond from Columbia I thought all things were smooth and pleasant once more. The woman's war at the Spotswood [hotel] was over, the belligerents dispersed; and Joe Johnston had gone West. Soon enough I found out my mistake. The Confederate Congress devoted the winter of 1862 to a hand-to-hand fight with Mr. Davis on account of Mr. Quartermaster General Myers. Then Northrop! What a bone of contention he is! Even if the army is mistaken, and Northrop is not inefficient, still something ought to be conceded to their prejudices. We need popular enthusiasm to take men triumphantly through such a martyrdom as life in camp surely is to them. **page 285/**

No. 88   John S. Wise, *The End of an Era,* Boston, Houghton, Mifflin and Company, 1902.

The United States laws relating to currency and revenue no longer obtained, and the Confederate laws had not been put into enforcement. The lack of small currency soon gave rise to the issue of one dollar and fifty-cent and twenty-five-cent bills, by nearly all the towns and counties of the State. Private bankers also issued these bills, and even private individuals. I remember particularly one Sylvester P. Cocke, an old fellow who had formerly kept a country store at Dover Mills, in Goochland County. In 1862, he had a little office upon the bank of the "Basin" or terminus of the James River and-Kanawha Canal, in Richmond. The office was not exceeding ten feet square, and stood in the corner of a large vacant coal-yard. Mr. Cocke's banking facilities consisted of a table, a small safe, a stack of sheets of bills, and a stout pair of shears. He had his I.O.U.'s printed on ordinary letter-paper. They had in one corner a picture of a mastiff lying in front of an iron safe, holding its key between his paws, and, besides the date, declared, "On demand I promise to pay to the bearer" one dollar, fifty cents, or twenty-five cents, or ten cents, and were **page 215/**   signed Sylvester P. Cocke in a clerical hand. There he sat signing, or clipping his promises apart with his shears, and although Mr. Cocke's means of redemption were an unknown factor, his notes passed current with people in Richmond, and all through the valley of the James, as if they had been obligations of the Bank of England. **page 216/**

No. 89 Mrs. D. Giraud Wright, *A Southern Girl in '61*, New York, Doubleday, Page & Company, 1905.

In this spirit of lightheartedness wrote the soldier boys from their camps in the mud and rain and discomfort of every kind. In Richmond too the young people managed to make merry, as young people will, under adverse circumstances. The girls made the best show possible with their meagre wardrobes — and fortunate were the extravagant ones of other days who had a multiplicity of garments, from which to levy supplies,   **page117/**   to cut and make over to suit the fashion of the day. On Franklin Street, on any fine afternoon during the winter, it was a lovely sight to watch the promenaders going up and down. The officers, on leave for a few days, made the best of their holiday, and the pretty girls were decked out in the best finery they could muster. The sun shone and hearts were light and the shadow of Appomattox was still so far away that not even the cloud as big as a man's hand had showed itself. The school girls too, in spite of the troublous times, found ways to amuse themselves. One day, when the snow lay thick on the ground, we were all at luncheon, when we heard a great shouting in the street, and with one accord rushed to the windows to see the cause. We found a regiment marching by, on their way through town, to the railway station. They were footsore and weary, ill clad and worse shod; but the flag was flying and they held their heads up and stepped out bravely, as the bevy of girls appeared on the doorsteps and greeted us with a great shout. We rushed in again and came out speedily, with our hands and aprons full of bread, and everything portable from the table. There was a halt, and we ran out in the street and passed on our refreshments from man to man. They laughed in great glee and cheered and shouted — and then such a frolic ensued, for one of the mischievous girls threw a snowball in their midst! This was "a   **page 118/** dare" and they took it! All discipline was at an end and the snowballs flew thick and fast — as they filed past us on their journey, alas! to battlefields from which many, indeed, most of them, would return no more. We went hungry till supper time; but were so glad to have cheered them on their weary way. **page 119/**

No. 90 Sallie A. Brock Putnam, *Richmond During the War*, New York, G. W. Carleton and Company, 1867.

[Winter of 1862-63:] As the war went on, a marked change was made in the educational interest of the South. For a certain   **page 188/**   number of pupils the teachers of schools were exempt from military duty. To their credit be it recorded that few, comparatively, availed themselves of this exception, and the care of instructing the youth devolved, with other added responsibilities, upon the women of the country. Only boys under the conscript age were found in the schools; all older were made necessary in the field or in some department of government service, unless physical inability prevented them from falling under the requirements of the law. Many of our colleges for males suspended operation, and in the most important period in the course of their education our youths were instructed in the sterner lessons of military service.

Female schools were supported as best they could be where there was a lamentable scarcity of books, and where the expenses of education were so great that only the most wealthy could afford to give their daughters the advantages of a liberal course. Such were the difficulties that hedged the way to mental cultivation, that it seemed, in many instances, almost a matter of impossibility to pursue any regular plan of education for girls.

The operations of the Richmond Female College were suspended, or rather, the building was given up for hospital purposes, and the excellent institution of Mr. LeFebvre was entirely broken up; but the Southern Female Institute, a first-grade seminary, under the supervision of Mr. Lee Powell, the fine school of Miss Pegram, St. Joseph's Academy, and other institutions under the patronage of the Catholic Church, were sustained. Though the encouragement to these schools was thoroughly liberal, so heavy were the expenses that it was almost impossible to keep them in successful operation.

There was also a sad want of school books. The stock on hand when the war commenced soon became exhausted, and there were no new ones to supply the consequent demand. Very few came to us through the blockade. Books were the last consideration in that eccentric trade. Inconveniences arose at every step to impede the progress of   page 189/   education in the Confederacy. School-books which had long before been cast aside as obsolete, and banished from the shelves of the library, and hidden away to moulder in dark closets, were brought to light, and placed in the hands of children, from which to add to the stock of ideas, in the process of youthful development.

There was no time for authorship or compilation, and publication was conducted under such serious disadvantages, and at such enormous cost, that it grew to be almost impossible. page 190/

No. 91 Mrs. D. Giraud Wright, *A Southern Girl in '61,* New York, Doubleday, Page & Company, 1905.

In reading over the letters written at this period (the Winter of '62-'63), the thing that strikes me is the tone of cheerfulness and hope that runs through all of them. It had not dawned yet on the minds of anyone that success was not assured. Jackson was the idol of the people and everything was anticipated of him when the spring campaign should open. The confidence in Lee was absolute; and no one doubted that he would carry all before him. The fact that provisions were scarce; that prices were phenomenally high; that the purchasing power of our currency was depreciating daily; seemed to make no impression on the temper or spirits of the people. At this time it was frequent for individuals to run the blockade, or come through the lines, and their advent was hailed with delight by their friends to whom they brought welcome presents in the shape of *shoes,* and other necessities, which it was difficult to procure in Richmond.   page 111/

The Virginia housekeeper, famed for her hospitality and good living, had hard work to produce a tempting ménu for her guests. It would have been droll (had the cause not been so tragic) to note the stress laid upon a fair supper, or the rare occasions when it was forthcoming. For they still had "parties," as they were called, and if, by good fortune, ice cream and cake and "real" coffee appeared, the delighted fact is duly recorded.   page 112/

1 8 6 3

*"There is life in the old land yet!"**

*Mary Boykin Chesnut, *A Diary from Dixie,* Boston, Houghton Mifflin Company, 1949, p. 341.

No. 92 Mrs. Roger A. Pryor, *Reminiscences of Peace and War,* New York, The Macmillan Company, 1905.

[Mrs. Pryor was the wife of Brigadier General and Congressman Roger A. Pryor. She spent most of the war period in Petersburg, her husband's home town. In her reminiscences, the most valuable information concerning Richmond in wartime appears in the form of letters sent to her from Richmond by "Agnes," a person whom she identifies only as a close friend.]

Richmond, January 7, 1863.

My Dearie: Have you no pen, ink, and paper on the Blackwater [Mrs. Pryor was at the General's camp here] — the very name of which suggests ink? I get no news of you at all. How do you amuse yourself and have you anything to read? I am sending you today a copy of Victor Hugo's last novel, "Les Miserables" reprinted by a Charleston firm on the best paper they could get, poor fellows, pretty bad I must acknowledge. You'll go wild over that book — I did — and everybody does.

. . . .

Do you realize the fact that we shall soon be without a stitch of clothes? There is not a bonnet for sale in Richmond. Some of the girls smuggle them, which I for one consider in the worst possible taste, to say the least. We have no right at this time to dress better than our neighbors, and besides, the soldiers need every cent of our money. Do you remember in Washington my pearl-gray silk bonnet, trimmed inside with lilies of the valley? I have ripped it up, washed and ironed it, dyed the lilies blue (they are bluebells now), and it is very becoming. All the girls intend to plait hats next summer when the wheat ripens, for they have no blocks on which to press the coal-scuttle bonnets, and after all when our blockade is raised we may find they are not at all worn, while hats are hats and never go out of fashion. The country girls made them last summer and pressed the crowns over bowls and tin pails. I could make lovely paper flowers if I had materials.

It seems rather volatile to discuss such things while our dear country is in such peril. Heaven knows I would costume myself in coffee-bags if that would help, but having no coffee, where could I get the bags? I'll e'en go afield next summer, and while Boaz is at the front, Ruth will steal the sheaves for her adornment.

The papers announce that General French reports the enemy forty-five thousand strong at Suffolk. How many men has your General? Dear, dear!

But we are fortifying around Richmond. While I write a great crowd of negroes is passing through the streets, singing as they march. They have been working on the fortifications north of the city, and are now going to work on them south of us. They don't seem to concern themselves much about Mr. Lincoln's Emancipation Proclamation, as they seem to have no desire to do any of the fighting.

Your loving

"Agnes."

P.S. — I attended Mrs. Davis's last reception. There was a crowd, all in evening dress. You see, as we don't often wear our evening gowns, they are still quite passable. I wore the gray silk with eleven flounces which was made   **page 227/** for Mrs. Douglas's last reception, and by the bye, who do you think was at the battle of Williamsburg, on General McClellan's staff? The Prince de Joinville who drank the rose wine with you at the Baron de Limbourg's reception to the Japs. Doesn't it all seem so long ago — so far away? The Prince de Joinville escorted me to one of the President's levees — don't you remember? — and now I attend another President's levee and hear him calmly telling some people that rats, if fat, are as good as squirrels, and that we can never afford mule meat. It would be too expensive, but the time may come when rats will be in demand.   **page 228/**

Dearly,

"Agnes."

No. 93   *Daily Richmond Examiner,* January 9, 1863, p. 1.

The Richmond Chess Club

We are glad to learn that this organization has survived the troubles and turmoils of the war and is now in prosperous condition, its membership being larger than at any previous period in its history. It is true that many of its ablest and most valued members are absent in the service of their country, but a sufficient number are always present to keep alive the organization, and make the club room one of the most interesting resorts in the city.

No. 94   John B. Jones, *A Rebel War Clerk's Diary,* New York, Old Hickory Bookshop, 1935, vol I (2 vols.).

February 11, 1863: Some idea may be formed of the scarcity of food in this city from the fact that, while my youngest daughter was in the kitchen today, a young rat came out of its hole and seemed to beg for something to eat; she held out some bread, which it ate from her hand, and seemed grateful. Several others soon appeared, and were as tame as kittens. Perhaps we shall have to eat them!   **page 257/**

No. 95   *Daily Richmond Examiner,* March 6, 1863, p. 1.

Worse and Worse

Not less than fourteen of the largest boarding houses in Richmond have closed their doors the present week to table boarders, on account of the scarcity and unprecedented high prices of all the necessaries of life, and more will follow their example soon.

At the large hotels the price of board and lodging per diem is six dollars, and if prices continue to advance in the same ratio in the future as they have in the past, boarding will advance to ten dollars a day.

No. 96 Judith W. McGuire, *Diary of a Southern Refugee*, New York, E. J. Hale & Son, 1867.

March 27, 1863: To-day was set apart by the President as a day of fasting and prayer. Some of us went to Richmond [at this time Mrs. McGuire was staying at Ashland] and joined in the services at St. Paul's. The churches were all crowded with worshippers, who, I trust, felt their dependence on God in this great struggle. The President was in church, and, I believe, most of the dignitaries. One of the ladies of the hospital, seeing this morning two rough-looking convalescent soldiers sitting by the stove, exhorted them to observe the day by prayer and fasting. They seemed to have no objection to the praying, but could not see the "good of fasting," and doubted very much whether "Marse Jeff fasted all day himself — do you reckon he does?" The lady laughingly told him that she would inquire and let them know, but she *reckoned* that such was his habit. In the course of the morning she met with Mrs. Davis and told her the anecdote. "Tell them from me," said Mrs. D., "that Mr. Davis never eats on fast-day, and **page 201/** that as soon as he returns from church he shuts himself up in his study, and is never interrupted during the day, except on public business." Of course this was soon given as an example, not only to the two convalescents, but to the whole hospital. **page 202/**

No. 97 Virginia Tunstall Clay, *A Belle of the Fifties*, New York, Doubleday, Page and Company, 1905.

> *[Senator and Mrs. Clay left Richmond in May, 1862, at the beginning of the Congressional recess. He returned on occasions in response to legislative duties, and she made several later stays of varying duration at Richmond, although the greater part of the two succeeding years was spent at the homes of hospitable kin "far away from the centre of anxiety and deprivation." The following is an excerpt from a letter which Mrs. Clay received from her husband in March, 1863.]*

"A general gloom prevails here because of the scarcity and high price of food. Our soldiers are on half-rations of meat, one-quarter pound of salt, and one-half pound of fresh meat, without vegetables, or fruit, or coffee or sugar! Don't mention this, as it will do harm to let it get abroad. Really there is a serious apprehension of having to disband part of the army for want of food. In this city the poor clerks and subaltern military officers are threatened with starvation, as they cannot get board on their pay. God only knows what is to become of us, if we do not soon drive the enemy from Tennessee and Kentucky and get food from their granaries. . . . I dined with the President yesterday at six P.M., *en famille,* on beef stew, beef soup, meat pie, potatoes, coffee, and bread. I approved his simple fare and expressed the wish that the army in the field had more to eat and that out of the field less"! **page 194/**

No. 98   Judith W. McGuire, *Diary of a Southern Refugee,* New York, E. J. Hale & Son, 1867.

April 2, 1863: We were shocked when the gentlemen returned, to hear of the riot which occurred in Richmond today. A mob, principally of women, appeared in the streets, attacking the stores. Their object seemed to be to get anything they could; dry-goods, shoes, brooms, meat, glassware, jewelry, were caught up by them. The military was called out — the Governor dispersed them from one part of **page 202/** the town, telling them that unless they disappeared in five minutes, the soldiers should fire among them. This he said, holding his watch in his hand. Mr. Mumford, the President of the Young Men's Christian Association, quieted them in another street, by inviting them to come to the rooms of the Association, and their wants should be supplied; many followed him — I suppose those who were really in want. Others there were, of the very worst class of women, and a great many who were not in want at all, which they proved by only supplying themselves with jewelry and other finery. The President was out speaking to them, and trying to secure order. The Mayor made them a speech, and seemed to influence them, but I dare say that the bayonets of the soldiers produced the most decided effect. It is the first time that such a thing has ever darkened the annals of Richmond. God grant it may be the last. I fear that the poor suffer very much; meal was selling today at $16 per bushel. It has been bought up by the speculators. Oh that these hard-hearted creatures could be made to suffer! Strange that men with human hearts can, in these dreadful times, thus grind the poor. **page 203/**

No. 99   Mrs. Roger A. Pryor, *Reminiscences of Peace and War,* New York, The Macmillan Company, 1905.

> *[Mrs. Pryor's friend "Agnes" could soon record graver things than idleness or gossip. On April 4, 1863, she wrote from Richmond: —]*

My Dear: I hope you appreciate the fact that you are herewith honored with a letter written in royal-red ink upon sumptuous gilt-edged paper. There is not, at present writing, one inch of paper for sale in the capital of the Confederacy, at all within the humble means of the wife of a Confederate officer. Well it is for her — and I hope for you — that her youthful admirers were few, and so her gorgeous cream-and-gold album was only half filled with tender effusions. Out come the blank leaves, to be divided between her friend and her Colonel. Don't be alarmed at the color of the writing. I have not yet dipped my goose-quill (there are no steel pens) in the 'ruddy drops that visit my sad heart,' nor yet into good orthodox red ink. There are fine oaks in the country, and that noble tree bears a gall-nut filled with crimson sap. One lies on my table, and into its sanguinary heart I plunge my pen.

Something very sad has just happened in Richmond — something that makes me ashamed of all my jeremiads over the loss of the petty comforts and conveniences of life — hats, bonnets, gowns, stationery, books, magazines, dainty food. . . .
page 237/

Yesterday, upon arriving, [at the Capitol Square] I found within the gates a crowd of women and boys — several hundreds of them, standing quietly together. I sat on a bench near, and one of the number left the rest and took the seat beside me. She was a pale, emaciated girl, not more than eighteen. . . . 'I could stand no longer,' she exclaimed. . . . As she raised her hand to remove her sunbonnet, her loose calico sleeve slipped up, and revealed a mere skeleton of an arm. She perceived my expression as I looked at it, and hastily pulled down her sleeve with a short laugh. 'This is all that's left of me!' she said. 'It seems real funny don't it?' . . . I was encouraged to ask: 'What is it? Is there some celebration?'

'There is,' said the girl, solemnly; 'we celebrate our right to live. We are starving. As soon as enough of us get together we are going to the bakeries and each of us will take a loaf of bread. That is little enough for the government to give us after it has taken all our men.'

Just then a fat old black Mammy waddled up the walk to overtake a beautiful child who was running before her. 'Come dis a way, honey,' she called, 'don't go nigh dem people,' adding in a lower tone, 'I's feared you'll ketch somethin' fum dem po'-white folks. I wonder dey lets 'em into de Park.'

The girl turned to me with a wan smile, as she rose to join the long line that now formed and was moving, she said simply, 'Good-by! I'm going to   page 238/ get something to eat!'

. . . The mob now rapidly increased, and numbered, I am sure, more than a thousand women and children. It grew and grew until it reached the dignity of a mob — a bread riot. They impressed all the light carts they met, and marched along silently and in order. They marched through Cary Street and Main, visiting the stores of the speculators and emptying them of their contents. Governor Letcher sent the Mayor to read the Riot Act, and as this had no effect he threatened to fire on the crowd. The city battalion then came up. The women fell back with frightened eyes, but did not obey the order to disperse. The President then appeared, ascended a dray, and addressed them. It is said that he was received at first with hisses from the boys, but after he had spoken some little time with great kindness and sympathy, the women quietly moved on, taking their food with them. . . . While I write women and children are still standing in the streets, demanding food, and the government is issuing to them rations of rice.

This is a frightful state of things. I am telling you of it because *not one word* has been said in the newspapers about it. All will be changed, Judge Campbell tells me, if we can win a battle or two (but, oh, at what a price!), and regain control of our railroads. Your General has been magnificent. He has fed Lee's army all winter — I wish he could feed our starving women and children.   page 239/

Dearly,

"Agnes"

No. 100 Varina Howell Davis, *Jefferson Davis*, New York, Belford Company, 1890, vol. II (2 vols.).

The steady depletion of the Confederate forces and the consequent success of the enemy, increased the sufferings of our people; suffering made them querulous, and they looked about to find the person to blame for their misfortune. Some of them found the culprit in the President. The most hopeful man might be expected to lose heart under this heavy load, but Mr. Davis's faith in God's interposition to protect the right never faltered, and he steadily followed the dictates of his conscience, nothing daunted by our misfortunes. Now a formidable manifestation in the form of a bread riot occurred in Richmond.

"On April 2, 1863, Mr. Davis said that he received word in his office that a serious disturbance, which the Mayor and Governor Letcher, with the State forces under his command, were entirely unable to repress, was in progress on the streets. He at once proceeded to the scene of trouble in the lower portion of the city, whither the venerable Mayor had preceded him. He found a large crowd on Main Street, although the mass of the rioters were congregated on one of the side streets leading into that thoroughfare. **page 373/** They were headed by a tall, daring Amazon-ian-looking woman, who had a white feather standing erect from her hat, and who was evidently directing the movement of the plunderers. The main avenue was blocked by a dray from which the horses had been taken, and which had been hauled across the street, and it was particularly noticeable that, though the mob claimed that they were starving and wanted bread, they had not confined their operations to food-supplies, but had passed by, without any effort to attack, several provision stores and bakeries, while they had completely emptied one jewelry store, and had also 'looted' some millinery and clothing shops in the vicinity. The fact was conclusive to the President's mind that it was not bread they wanted, but that they were bent on nothing but plunder and wholesale robbery.

"At the Confederate Armory in Richmond were engaged a number of armorers and artisans enrolled by General Gorgas, chief of ordnance, to work especially for the Government. These men had been organized into a military company under the command of a captain whose bearing was that of a trained, sturdy officer accustomed to obey orders, and ready to do his duty unflinchingly, no matter what it might be. This company had been **page 374/** promptly ordered to the scene of the riot and arrived shortly after the President.

"Mr. Davis mounted the dray above mentioned and made a brief address to the formidable crowd of both sexes, urging them to abstain from their lawless acts. He reminded them of how they had taken jewelry and finery instead of supplying themselves with bread, for the lack of which they claimed they were suffering. He concluded by saying: 'You say you are hungry and have no money. Here is all I have; it is not much, but take it.' He then, emptying his pockets, threw all the money they contained among the mob, after which he took out his watch and said:

'We do not desire to injure anyone, but this lawlessness must stop. I will give you five minutes to disperse, otherwise you will be fired on.' The order was given the company to prepare for firing, and the grim, resolute old Captain — who, Mr. Davis says, was an old resident of Richmond, but whose name he does not recall — gave his men the command: 'Load!' The muskets were then loaded with buck and ball cartridges, with strict observance of military usage, and everyone could see that when this stern commander received orders to fire he intended to shoot to kill. The mob evidently fully realized this fact, and at once   page 375/   began to disperse, and before the five minutes had expired the trouble was over, and the famous misnamed bread riot was at an end."

This is a succinct and truthful account of this trouble, which created so much excitement at the time, and of the part which ex-President Davis bore therein. The subject having been recently revived and extensively discussed, and quite a variety of statements having been made in connection therewith, this accout of Mr. Davis will be read with great interest, and all who personally remember the scenes and incidents of that memorable occasion will no doubt fully substantiate its correctness. page 376/

No. 101 Ernest Taylor Walthall, *Hidden Things Brought to Light,* Richmond, Va., The Dietz Printing Co., 1933.

> [The Apologia of this book reads: In putting "Hidden Things Brought to Light" into type my idea was to stamp my memory on paper and present it to the older men in the city to see if my memory was correct. I used no notes, simply set the type as my memory flowed, and printed it page at a time. Thus you will see my grammar is not smooth, nor the orthography correct. Only 15 or 20 copies were printed and the proofs were never corrected.]

I saw the Bread Riot led by Mrs. Jackson, a painter's wife. Just as I reached Parr and Keesee's, at 12th and Cary, they were coming out with hams and other eatibles. There was a hatchet in someones hands, from the blood that flowed from Mr. Tyler. On to Old Market I hurried, there to meet Captain Gay, with the Public Guard, telling that gathering of women, some who were the wives, sisters and daughters of the men before them who are ready to see that law and order are preserved. Women, if you don't disburse and quietly scatter (the cartridges were filled with a ball and 2 buckshot; but Gay, knowing the women, became nervous), I order to put "two balls and a buckshot into you."   page 24/

No. 102 Ernest Taylor Walthall, *Hidden Things Brought to Light,* Richmond, Va., The Dietz Printing Co., 1933.

Don't sensure that wild, starving, clothless crowd. Don't call them a mob of robbers and inscendaries. Think of it, those people, certainly for three years had deprived themselves of the very thing before them, now without price or money, knowing not where their next meal would come from or how they would be able to cloth themselves unless that was the very raven God had sent. You will be surprised when you know a good man as Bishop Dogget was there picking up what would be useful.   page 32/

No. 103   *Official Records of the Union and Confederate Armies, series* I, volume XVIII, Washington, Government Printing Office, 1902.

Richmond, April 2, 1863.

W. S. Morris, Esq.,
    President Telegraph Company:

I am desired by the Secretary of War to request that you will permit nothing relative to the unfortunate disturbance which occurred in the city today to be sent over the telegraph lines in any direction for any purpose.   page 958/

Very respectfully, &c.,

JNO. WITHERS,
Assistant Adjutant-General.

No. 104   *Official Records of the Union and Confederate Armies, series* I, volume XVIII, Washington, Government Printing Office, 1902.

Richmond, April 2, 1863.

To the Richmond Press:

GENTLEMEN: The unfortunate disturbance which occurred today in this city is so liable to misconstruction and misrepresentation abroad that I am desired by the Secretary of War to make a special appeal to the editors and reporters of the press at Richmond, and earnestly request them to avoid all reference directly or indirectly to the affair. The reasons for this are so obvious that it is unnecessary to state them, and the Secretary indulges the hope that his own views in this connection will be approved of by the press generally. Any other course must tend to embarrass our cause, and to encourage our enemies in their inhuman policy.   page 958/

Very respectfully, &c.,

JNO. WITHERS,
Assistant Adjutant-General.

No. 105 Sallie A. Brock Putnam, *Richmond During the War,* New York, G. W. Carleton and Company, 1867.

The real sufferers were not of the class who would engage in acts of violence to obtain bread, but included the most worthy and highly cultivated of our citizens, who, by the suspension of the ordinary branches of business, and the extreme inflation in the prices of provisions, were often reduced to abject suffering; and helpless refugees, who, driven from comfortable homes, were compelled to seek relief in the crowded city, at the time insufficiently furnished with the means of living for the resident population, and altogether inadequate to the increased numbers thrown daily into the progress of events. How great their necessities must have been can be imagined from the fact that many of our women, reared in the utmost ease, delicacy and refinement, were compelled to dispose of all articles of taste and former luxury, and frequently necessary articles of clothing to meet the necessary demands of life.

These miseries and inconveniences were submitted to in no fault-finding spirit; and although the poverty of the masses increased from day to day, there is no doubt that the sympathies of the people were unfalteringly with the revolution in all its phases. page 210/

No. 106 *Official Records of the Union and Confederate Armies,* series IV, volume II, Washington, Government Printing Office, 1902.

Executive Department,
Tallahassee, April 15, 1863.

His Excellency Jefferson Davis,
Richmond, Va.:

. . . .

I believe now the wisest and best course which existing circumstances suggest to prevent the planting of excessive crops, insure the culture of cereals, sustain the public credit, prevent speculation, extortion, and riots for bread — a measure entirely consistent with constitutional liberty, conducive to the general welfare, and to the independence of the Confederate States — would be an act of Congress prohibiting, under severe penalties, all commercial intercourse with foreign nations, except such as should be authorized by the Government through special agents, and exclusively for the purposes of Government. If trade between our citizens and the speculators who succeed in running the blockade was prevented, all inducements to make cotton except for the benefit of the Goverment in its negotiations and for domestic uses would be cut off; individual energy and enterprise and enlightened public sentiment would insure the necessities and even the comforts of life to the people and to the armies; the Confederate currency would be independent in itself for all the purposes of commerce between the States, individuals, and the Confederate Government, as there would be no demand for specie or foreign exchange to sustain our domestic commerce. Thus inducements to speculation and extortion would be destroyed, our people would depend on themselves, and the Confederate Government would reflect the intelligence and probity of an independent and self-sustaining association of States. **page 489/**

.   .   .   .

I have the honor to be, respectfully,

John Milton
Governor of Florida

No. 107   John B. Jones, *A Rebel War Clerk's Diary*, New York, Old Hickory Bookshop, 1935, vol. I (2 vols.).

April 17, 1863: Pins are so scarce and costly, that it is now a pretty general practice to stoop down and pick up any found in the street. The boarding houses are breaking up, and rooms, furnished and unfurnished, are rented out to messes. One dollar and fifty cents for beef, leaves no margin for profit, even at $100 per month, which is charged for board, and most of the boarders cannot afford to pay that price. Therefore they take rooms, and buy their own scanty food. I am inclined to think provisions would not be deficient, to an alarming extent, if they were equally distributed. Wood is no scarcer than before the war, and yet $30 per load (less than a cord) is demanded for it, and obtained. **page 294/**

No. 108   John B. Jones, *A Rebel War Clerk's Diary*, New York, Old Hickory Bookshop, 1935, vol. I (2 vols.).

May 2, 1863: . . . There is no such thing as fear, in this community, of personal danger, even among the women and **page 305/** children; but there is some alarm by the opulent inhabitants, some of whom, for the sake of their property, would submit to the invader. One thing is pretty certain, Richmond will not fall by assault without costing the lives of 50,000 men, which is about equal to its population in ordinary times.

Well, I am planting potatoes in my little garden, and hope to reap the benefit of them. I pay 50 cts. per quart for seed potatoes, and should be chagrined to find my expenditure of money and labor had been for the benefit of the invader! Yet it may be so; and if it should be, still there are other little gardens to cultivate where we might fly to. We have too broad and too long a territory in the revolted States to be overrun and possessed by the troops of the United States. **page 306/**

No. 109 John B. Jones, *A Rebel War Clerk's Diary*, New York, Old Hickory Bookshop, 1935, vol. I (2 vols.).

May 10, 1863: Detachments of Federal troops are now marching into the city every few hours, guarded by (mostly) South Carolinians, dressed in home-spun, dyed yellow with the bark of the butter-nut tree. Yesterday evening, at 7 o'clock, a body of 2000 arrived, being marched in by way of the Brooke Pike, near to my residence. Only 200 Butternuts had them in charge, and a less number would have sufficed, for they were extremely weary. Some of them however, attempted to be humorous.

A young officer asked one of the spectators if the "Libby" (the prison) was the best house in the city to put up at. He was answered that it was the best *he* would find.

Another passed some compliment on a mulatto wench, who replied: "Go long, you nasty Abolition Yankee."

One of our soldiers taken at Arkansas Post, just exchanged, walked along with the column, and kept repeating these words: "Now you know how *we* felt when you marched us through your cities."

But generally a deep silence was maintained, and neither insult nor dignity offered the fallen foe. Other columns are on the way — and how they are to be subsisted is a vexatious question. **page 318/**

No. 110 *Daily Richmond Examiner,* May 12, 1863, p. 2.

Reception of the Remains of General T. J. Jackson

Richmond, the Capital of the Confederacy, and the Commonwealth of Virginia, yesterday received into its great heart, bursting with grief, the mortal remains of her gallant son, and the nation's hero and hope, General T. J. Jackson, a name henceforth immortal. Had a visible pall overspread the city, it would not have expressed grief more profound, nor sorrow more universal than that which fired every heart, and sat upon every countenance. It was as though death had come home to every household, and snatched the one dearest away.

The recommendation of the Mayor, closing places of business after 10 o'clock, A.M., was generally complied with, and flags on the public buildings of the State and Confederate Government floated at half-mast, and the Departments, State and Confederacy, were also closed after 12 M. . . . Shortly after four o'clock, the special train, bearing the remains, was announced, and drove slowly up into the depot, the bells of the city meanwhile sending their solemn peals over the city, and into the thousands of throbbing hearts. The coffin, containing the remains, was removed from the car, and enshrouded with the flag under which the Christian hero fought and fell, and covered with spring flowers, placed upon the hearse in waiting. . . . The cortege moved, the band playing the "Dead March," and entering the Capitol Square, by the main gateway on Ninth, proceeded direct to the front of the Governor's Mansion. . . . During the moving of the pageant from the depot to the Governor's Mansion the exhibitions of the public grief were frequent and unrestrained. Tears stood in the eyes of stern men and gentle women, as they gazed upon the coffin, as though they doubted that it contained in its narrow space, the remains of one who was at once so great, so true, and so beloved. . . . This morning the body, prepared and enclosed in a metallic case, will be laid in state in the Capitol, previous to the removal to Lexington, Virginia, the spot to be consecrated a Mecca and a shrine in after generations by his grave.

No. 111 Elizabeth Wright Weddell, *St. Paul's Church, Its Historic Years and Memorials*, Richmond, Virginia, The William Byrd Press, 1931, vol. 1 (2 vols.).

> *[From the report on the "State of the Church" delivered by Charles Minnigerode, D.D., Third Rector of St. Paul's Church, 1863.]*

To our ministers, especially at this crisis, we would say, what is wanted is not sermons on the times and the war and the objects of our country's hopes. We need not preach to the soldiers about war and camp and battles; they hear and think enough of that without our help. What they want and expect of us, as ministers of Christ, is just the glad tidings of salvation, just the eternal message of grace and love to perishing sinners. We venture to say that no chaplain, and no missionary, to the army or to hospitals will do their work efficiently and faithfully unless they speak as to immortal souls, standing face to face with God; unless they preach Christ and Him crucified, the power of God unto salvation to those who believe.   **page 193/**

No. 112 *Daily Richmond Examiner*, May 25, 1863, p. 1.

The Public Health

The season is now upon us when the lanes and alleys of the city should receive from the police the strictest immediate attention, else the mass of refuse matter and decayed vegetation will breed disease as sure as the sun shines. All the by-ways and alleys of the city have not experienced a cleansing since last summer, when the apprehension of contagion and fever induced the authorities to give them a purifying. To arrest the evils of disease, attention to the nuisances of the city should be given at once, and thoroughly carried out.

No. 113 Constance Cary Harrison, *Recollections, Grave and Gay,* New York, Charles Scribner's Sons, 1912.

Our most illustrious caller that spring [1863] was the commander-in-chief of the Army of Northern Virginia. General Lee came one evening, and after a pleasant talk with my mother and me, arose to go, we escorting him to the front door. It was broad moonlight, and I recall as if it were yesterday the superb figure of our hero standing in the little porch without, saying a few last words as he swung his military cape around his shoulders. It did not need my fervid imagination to think him the most noble looking mortal I had ever seen. As he swept off his hat for a second and final farewell, he bent down and kissed me as he often did the girls he had known from their childhood. At that time General Lee was literally the idol of the Confederacy. His moral grandeur, recognized by all, lifted him into the region where "Envy, nor calumny, nor hate, nor pain" did not venture to assail him. We felt, as he left us and walked off up the quiet leafy street in the moonlight, that we had been honored as by more than royalty.

We went often to Mrs. Davis's receptions, where the President never failed to say kind words in passing, and sometimes to tarry for a pleasant chat. Always grave, always looking as if he bore the sorrows of a world, he was invariably courteous and sometimes playful in his talk with very young women. These entertainments of Mrs. Davis's, in the evening between limited hours, were attended by every one not in deep mourning. The lady of the Confederate White House, while not always sparing of witty sarcasms upon those who had affronted page 127/ her, could be depended upon to conduct her salon with extreme grace and convenient ease. Her sister, Margaret Howell, aided to lend it brilliancy. page 128/

No. 114 The *Record,* Richmond, Virginia, June 18, 1863, p. 5.

An Act to Authorize the Formulation of Volunteer Companies for Local Defense

The Congress of the Confederate States do enact, that for the purpose of local defense in any portion of the Confederate States, any number of persons not less than twenty, who are over the age of forty-five years, or otherwise not liable to military duty, may associate themselves as a military company, elect their own officers, and establish rules and regulations for their own government, and shall be considered as belonging to the provisional army of the Confederate States, serving without pay or allowances, and entitled, when captured by the enemy, to all privileges of prisoners of war. (Approved October 13, 1862)

No. 115   *Daily Richmond Examiner,* July 3, 1863, p. 2.

Richmond was magnificent yesterday. At ten o'clock the alarm bell sounded, and an official announcement was made that battle between the Yankee army of the Peninsula and the Confederate troops was imminent. Having an assurance that their service in the field would be useful, the whole male population of the place poured at once into the Square, were properly armed with the regulation rifle, were formed into regiments, and were marched to the fortifications. Rich and poor, old and young, the eminences of the learned profession, and the unlettered daily laborer, marched side by side, eagerly ready and eager to do all that were required of them. It was a noble thing to see. There was no possibility of doubting the reality, and the community, of the determination to fight for home which animated the people. . . .

The battle which they confidently expected to make for Richmond unfortunately could not be made, for the solid reason that the Yankee columns could not be enticed within fifteen miles of the Confederate outer works; having, perhaps, ascertained that, besides the militia, there were few more than "four thousand" regulars in the neighborhood of Richmond.

No. 116   *Daily Richmond Examiner,* July 6, 1863, p. 1.

Vaccination

Since the appearance of the small pox in Richmond, the authorities have been energetic in their efforts to procure the vaccination of every soldier and other persons in the employ of the Government.

No. 117   John B. Jones, *A Rebel War Clerk's Diary,* New York, Old Hickory Bookshop, 1935, vol. I (2 vols.).

July 22, 1863: Col. Northrop, Commissary General, sends in a paper to-day saying that only a quarter of a pound of meat per day can be given to the soldiers, except when marching, and then only half a pound. He says no more can be derived from the trans-Mississippi country, nor from the State of Mississippi, or Tennessee, and parts of Georgia and Alabama; and if more than the amount he receives be given the soldiers, the negroes will have to go without any. He adds, however, that the peasants of Europe rarely have to eat meat, and in Hindostan [sic], never. **page 385/**

No. 118 Mrs. D. Giraud Wright, *A Southern Girl in '61*, New York, Doubleday, Page & Company, 1905.

It is curious to note how youth will extract gayety and pleasure out of adverse surroundings. I find recorded in letters at this time [summer of 1863], in spite of the gnawing anxieties which were weighing down the hearts of all serious people, that sundry delightful parties were organized to partake of strawberries and ice cream at "Pizzini's," the famous confectioners of the day in Richmond. Expeditions were planned to Drewry's Bluff with a band of music in attendance, and, of course, with the usual accompaniment of the delightful officer, who, equally, of course, was either halt, lame or blind, as all whole men were at their posts in the field in June, 1863. Serenades, too, were in order, and I find that on our return from one of the aforesaid strawberry feasts, about twelve o'clock on the same night Ella —— had a charming serenade of a *full brass band* from one of her   **page 135/**   admirers. This combination of serenade, with strawberries and ice cream, seemed to fill the cup of joy to the brim.   **page 136/**

No. 119 Judith W. McGuire, *Diary of a Southern Refugee*, New York, E. J. Hale & Son, 1867.

July 28, 1863: The girls [Mrs. McGuire's] are in Richmond, staying at Dr. G's. **page 233/** They went in to attend a tournament to be given today by General Jenkin's Brigade, stationed near Richmond; but this morning the brigade was ordered to go South, and great was the disappointment of the young people. They cannot feel as we do during these gloomy times, but are always ready to catch the "passing pleasure as it flies," forgetting that in the best times,
> Pleasures are like poppies spread:
> You seize the flower, the bloom is shed.

And how much more uncertain are they now, when we literally cannot tell what a day may bring forth, and none of us know, when we arise in the morning, that we may not hear before noonday that we have been shorn of all that makes life dear! **page 234/**

No. 120 The *Record*, Richmond, Virginia, August 20, 1863, p. 91.

The first sixteen days of August, throughout the country, were marked by an intensity of heat rarely experienced for so long a period. Careful observation of the thermometer at various hours during this time, induces us to believe that at no hour of the day or night did the mercury fall below 80° of Fahrenheit.

No. 121 Mrs. D. Giraud Wright, *A Southern Girl in '61,* New York, Doubleday, Page & Company, 1905.

At this time [fall of 1863] the deepest anxiety was felt for the success of our cause in the West — and my father's [Senator Louis T. Wigfall of Texas] advocacy of General J. E. Johnston's being given control of affairs in that department was earnest and persistent. But it was disregarded by the President; and led to a severance of their friendly relations. While he never varied in his estimate of the President's sincerity, integrity and patriotism, nor ceased to admire the pure and noble character of the man — he never could justify his absolute refusal to waive his private judgment in the crisis of his country's trial and hearken to the appeals of men whose patriotism and judgment he should have regarded as certainly equals of his own. That he erred, erred fatally, no one cognizant of the state of affairs at the time can doubt; but it is equally sure that the penalty of his mistakes was borne with a dignity and serene courage which excited the admiration **page 159/** of the world. In modern times there has been no such spectacle as that frail old man, the chief magistrate of eight millions of people, lying manacled in a dungeon, bearing vicariously the sufferings and penalties of his people! He may have erred — but when the fetters were placed upon him the Southern people forgot everything but that he was their first and only President.   **page 160/**

No. 122 William Best Hesseltine, *Civil War Prisons, Columbus,* The Ohio State University Press, 1930.

[The bad conditions which existed during the winter of 1863-64] in the prisons in Richmond had been foreseen by General Robert E. Lee as early as October, 1863. Learning from the papers that the Federal Government had decided to make no further exchanges, Lee wrote to Secretary Seddon suggesting that prisoners not be held in Richmond. He declared that the city was not a good place for prisoners since their retention there would increase the amount of supplies to be transported. The already inadequate   **page 129/**   transportation system, in his opinion, should be devoted entirely to the needs of the citizens. Prisoners would cause higher prices and consequent distress among the poorer classes. The prisoners were also a danger from a military standpoint in that they gave aid and information to the enemy and would endanger the city in case of an attack. **page 130/**

No. 123 John B. Jones, *A Rebel War Clerk's Diary*, New York, Old Hickory Bookshop, 1935, vol. II (2 vols.).

October 24, 1863: A private note from General Lee, dated the 13th instant, which I saw today, informs the Secretary of War that much of the benefits he anticipated from his movement, then in progress, must be lost, from the fact that the enemy had been informed of his purposes. This it was the duty of the government to prevent, but Mr. Seddon, like his predecessors, cannot be convinced that the rogues and cut-throats employed by Gen. Winder as detectives, have it in their power to inflict injury on the cause and the country. The cleaning of the Augean stables here is the work which should engage the attention of the Secretary of War, rather than directing the movements of armies in the field, of which matter he knows nothing whatever.   **page 81/**

No. 124 George Cary Eggleston, *A Rebel's Recollections*, New York, G. P. Putnam's Sons, 1905.

At one time, when General Stuart, with his cavalry, was encamped within a few miles of the city, he discovered that his men were visiting Richmond by dozens, **page 220/** without leave, which, for some reason or other known only to the provost marshal's office, they were able to do without molestation. General Stuart, finding that this was the case, resolved to take the matter into his own hands, and accordingly with a troop of cavalry he made a descent upon the theatre one night, and arrested those of his men whom he found there. The provost marshal, who it would seem was more deeply concerned for the preservation of his own dignity than for the maintenance of discipline, sent a message to the great cavalier, threatening him with arrest if he should again presume to enter Richmond for the purpose of making arrests. Nothing could have pleased Stuart better. He replied that he should visit Richmond again the next night, with thirty horsemen; that he should patrol the streets in search of absentees from his command; and that General Winder might arrest him if he could. The jingling of spurs was loud in **page 221/** the streets that night, but the provost marshal made no attempt to arrest the defiant horseman.   **page 222/**

No. 125   Mary Boykin Chesnut, *A Diary from Dixie*, Boston, Houghton Mifflin Company, 1949.

December 4, 1863: I bought yesterday at the Commissary's one barrel of flour, one bushel of potatoes, one peck of rice, five pounds of salt beef, and one peck of salt, all for fifty dollars. In the street, a barrel of flour sells for one hundred and fifteen dollars.   **page 329/**

No. 126   John B. Jones, *A Rebel War Clerk's Diary*, New York, Old Hickory Bookshop, 1935, vol. II (2 vols.).

December 9, 1863: The President's message [to Congress] is not regarded with much favor by the croakers. The long complaint against foreign   **page 112/**   powers for not recognizing us is thought in bad taste, since all the points nearly had been made in a previous message. They say it is like abusing society for not admitting one within its circle as well as another. The President specifies no plan to cure the redundancy of the currency. He is opposed to increasing the pay of the soldiers, and absolutely reproaches the soldiers on the left wing of Bragg's army with not performing their whole duty in the late battle [Lookout Mountain].

Mr. Foote denounced the President today. He said he had striven to keep silent, but could not restrain himself while his State was bleeding — our disasters being all attributable by him to the President, who retained incompetent or unworthy men in command, etc.   **page 113/**

No. 127   T. C. DeLeon, *Four Years in Rebel Capitals*, Mobile, Alabama, The Gossip Printing Company, 1890.

No department was worse neglected and mismanaged than [the transportation department]. The existence of the Virginia army wholly depended on a single line, close to the coast and easily tapped. Nor did Government's seizure of its control, in any manner remedy the evil. Often and again, the troops around Richmond were without beef — once for twelve days at a time; they were often without flour, molasses or salt, living for days upon cornmeal alone! and the ever-ready excuse was want of transportation.

Thousands of bushels of grain would ferment and rot at one station; hundreds of barrels of meat stacked at another, while the army starved because of "no transportation!" But who recalls the arrival of a blockader at Charleston, Savannah, or Wilmington, when its ventures were not exposed at the auctions of Richmond, in time unreasonably short!   **page 281/**

No. 128 Constance Cary Harrison, *Recollections, Grave and Gay,* New York, Charles Scribner's Sons, 1912.

. . . The ladies of General Lee's family lived in a pleasant house in lower Franklin Street, then and afterward held as a shrine in the eyes of patriotic pilgrims. Mrs. Robert E. Lee, not strong in health and always a reserved woman in society, rarely showed herself in general gatherings. Miss Mary Custis Lee, who has for years been known to the exclusive circles of foreign capitals, having spent most of her later life abroad, took the post of receiving and entertaining the friends and admirers who thronged around their doors. The death of a beloved daughter during the war, followed by that of Mrs. Fitzhugh Lee and her children, while her husband was in prison in the North, placed the family in mourning, disqualifying them for conspicuous appearance in society. Also, it was understood that Mrs. Lee felt a sense of impropriety in the suggestion that the wife and daughters of the commanding general of half-starved armies, himself sleeping always in a tent and living on ascetic fare, should take the lead in any entertainments of a social sort; so the old elegant hospitality of Arlington House, which had opened its doors to so many in the past, was allowed to pass **page 153/** away, to be renewed, however, at their future home in Lexington. **page 154/**

No. 129 T. C. DeLeon, *Four Years in Rebel Capitals,* Mobile, Alabama, The Gossip Printing Company, 1890.

An examination of the leading journals of the South of this period will show that — whatever their mismanagement and want of business success — there was no lack of ability in their editorial columns. Such organs as the New Orleans *Delta,* Mobile *Advertiser,* Charleston *Mercury* and Richmond *Examiner* and *Whig* might have taken rank alongside of the best-edited papers of the country. Their literary ability was, perhaps, greater than that of the North; their discussions of the questions of the hour were clear, strong, and scholarly, and possessed, besides, the invaluable quality of honest conviction. Unlike the press of the North, the southern journals were not hampered by any business interests; they were unbiased, unbought and free to say what they thought and felt. And say it they did, in the boldest and plainest of language.

Nowhere on the globe was the freedom of the press more thoroughly vindicated than in the Southern States of America. And during the whole course of the war, criticisms of men and measures were constant and outspoken. So much so, indeed, that in many instances the operations of the Government were embarrassed, or the action of a department commander seriously hampered, by hostile criticisms in a newspaper. In naval operations, and the workings of the Conscript Law, especially was the freedom felt to be injurious; and though it sprang from the perfectly pure motive of doing the best for the cause — though the smallest southern journal, printed on straw paper and with worn-out type, was above purchase, or hush money — still it might have been better at times had gag-law been applied. **page 289/**

No. 130 Mrs. D. Giraud Wright, *A Southern Girl in '61*, New York, Doubleday, Page & Company, 1905.

The winter of '63-'64 saw us back in Richmond. The Army of Northern Virginia was inactive during the latter part of the winter but made a campaign of heroic endurance without parallel, for suffering and privation. With no proper shelter, half clothed, many without shoes, and barely enough food to keep away starvation, they bore the rigors of the season, the cold rains and snows, the dreary days and long nights of discomfort with no blankets to cover them, without a murmur. The currency was now so depreciated that the pay of the highest officers was inadequate for their wants. With cornmeal at $50 a bushel; beans at $60; bacon at $8 and sugar at $20 a pound it was almost impossible to procure the necessaries of life in Richmond — and yet I do not **page 165/** remember during that winter of suffering and anxiety, ever to have heard the eventual success of our cause questioned. The spirits of the people generally were bright and buoyant. The question of clothes became a burning one, and many were the devices resorted to in order to meet the needs of the occasion. Early in March Dahlgren's raid around Richmond took place and struck terror into the hearts of the women and children when the character of the orders captured on his person were known. It was stated and believed at the time that he and his command had *volunteered* for this expedition. He was repulsed and lost his life in the attempt, which resulted in absolute failure. The orders found on his person were explicit, and most extraordinary, when viewed in the light of the usual rules governing civilized warfare. He was ordered to burn the city of Richmond, and the oakum and turpentine to carry out this purpose were found with him. He was ordered to sack and loot the city, then filled with helpless women and children — and to the mercy of God we owe it that he was prevented from carrying out his purpose, and that an awful crime against civilization and humanity was not committed. My father said at the time, and I have lived to see his prophecy come true, that in future years no one would believe that such orders had been given or such an expedition organized, but these are facts nevertheless. All during that early spring the alarms in Richmond of an attack on the city were **page 166/** frequent; and at any hour of the day or night would be heard the sound of the alarm bells ringing and all the remaining men in the town, the clerks and civil officers, would gather up their arms and rally to the defence of their homes and the protection of their families. It was a wretched time of anxiety almost unbearable. **page 167/**

1 8 6 4

"... *the old brilliancy and fire were fast ebbing away.*"*

*"An Evening with the Venerable Statesman and Jurist, Hon. Thomas J. Semmes," *Southern Historical Society Papers*, vol. XXV, p. 331.

1864

No. 131 The Richmond *Enquirer,* January 2, 1864, p. 2.

Living in 1864

There was the same extent of excitement among the people on yesterday concerning the hiring rates as there was a day or two ago on the substitute question. To many the sudden increase in the prices for service was absolutely shocking, and the plan of deviating into the experiment of doing without the irrepressible nigger was discussed with considerable freedom. — For servant men, as dining room waiters and the like, owners asked from $500 to $700 — the larger number, however, being from $500 to $600. Boys for similar service, commanded from $200 to $450. First rate cooks were offered at from 400 to 700. Girls $200 to $400. To these rates is added the usual obligation of the one who hires to furnish clothing, and also to board the servant. It is very plain, therefore, that numerous families will begin to induct the young, half-grown scions of their respective houses into the mysteries of cooking and housekeeping, and many an amiable young creature will find herself waiting-maid, as well as mistress, of her own apartment, and probably of two or three others besides; while Mr. John and his worthy co-mates of the hobbledehoy stage of existence, will be taught the uses of adversity at the wood pile and the coal cellar, and in getting up at six in the morning to light the kitchen fire, black his own boots, and "tote" the water.

We will venture to say that there is not a white man or woman, old or young in this community, dependent upon a stated salary alone for his or her support, who does more than secure subsistence and clothing, and if the owners of slaves were considerate they would not expect *very much more* for their ebo-shins [ebo-skins?].

The hotel keepers have already taken up the tune, and advanced the rates of board at from $12 to $15 per day — brought about principally by the doubled and trebled prices they now have to pay for servants, and, of course, the prospect of a speedy advance upon everything else. The boarding house keepers, to a great extent, have also notified their boarders that henceforth from $40 to $80 per week will cover the ordinary expenses at their respective establishments, and nothing less.

House rent is on the same scoot upwards. We met a man yesterday whose heart was almost broken because he had met another man a few minutes before, who had offered him $3,500 a year for one of his houses, and he had pledged it two months ago for $2,000 to a poor lady from the South.

No. 132 Varina Howell Davis, *Jefferson Davis,* New York, Belford Company, 1890, vol. II (2 vols.), p. 534.

Travelling Expenses of an Officer of Artillery en route from Richmond, Va., to Augusta, Ga., March and April, 1865.

March 11th,	Meal on the road	$20.00
" 17th,	Cigars and Bitters	$60.00
" 20th,	Hair-cutting and shave	$10.00
" "	Pair of eye-glasses	$135.00
" "	Candles	$50.00
" 23d,	Coat, vest, and pants	$2700.00
" 27th,	One gallon whiskey	$400.00
" 30th,	One pair of pants	$700.00
" "	One pair of cavalry boots	$450.00
April 12th,	Six yards of linen	$1200.00
" 14th,	One ounce sul. quinine	$1700.00
" "	Two weeks' board	$700.00
" "	Bought $60, gold	$6000.00
" 24th,	One dozen Catawba wine	$900.00
" "	Shad and sundries	$75.00
" "	Matches	$25.00
" "	Penknife	$125.00
" "	Package Brown Windsor	$50.00

Prices on a Bill of Fare at the Oriental Restaurant, Richmond, January 17, 1864

Soup, per plate	$1.50		*Wines, per Bottle.*	
Turkey, per plate	3.50		Champagne	$50.00
Chicken, per plate	3.50		Madeira	50.00
Rock fish, per plate	5.00		Port	25.00
Roast beef, per plate	3.00		Claret	20.00
Beefsteak, per plate	3.50		Sherry	35.00
Ham and Eggs	3.50		*Liquors, per Drink.*	
Boiled eggs	2.00		French Brandy	3.00
Fried oysters	5.00		Rye whiskey	2.00
Raw oysters	3.00		Apple brandy	2.00
Cabbage	1.00		*Malt Liquors, per Bottle.*	
Potatoes	1.00		Porter	12.00
Pure coffee, per cup	3.00		Ale	12.00
Pure tea, per cup	2.00		Ale, one-half bottle	6.00
Fresh milk	2.00		*Cigars.*	
Bread and Butter	1.50		Fine Havana	1.00

Game of all kinds in season

Terrapins served up in every style

No. 133 Varina Howell Davis, *Jefferson Davis*, New York, Belford Company, 1890, vol. II (2 vols.), p. 535.

Bill for a Dinner for Nine Poor Confederates at the "Oriental," January 17, 1864

Soup for nine	$13.50	Brought forward	$132.50
Venison steak	31.50	Apples	12.00
Fried potatoes	9.00	5 bottles of Madeira	250.00
Seven birds	24.00	6 bottles of Claret	120.00
Baked potatoes	9.00	1 Urn cocktail	65.00
Celery	13.50	Jelly	20.00
Bread and Butter	14.00	Cake	20.00
Coffee	18.00	1 dozen cigars	12.00
	$132.50		$631.50

Approximate Value of Gold and Confederate Currency from January 1, 1862, to April 12, 1865

DATE	GOLD	CURRENCY
January 1, 1862	$100	$120
December 20, 1862	100	300
December 20, 1863	100	1,700
January 1, 1864	100	1,800
December 20, 1864	100	2,800
January 1, 1865	100	3,400
February 1, 1865	100	5,000
March 1, 1865	100	4,700
April 10, 1865	100	5,500

No. 134 *Southern Historical Society Papers*, Richmond, Virginia, 1876-1943, vol. XXV (49 vols.).

[*The following are excerpts from an article written for the* Picayune *by an unidentified person about his visit with Mr. Semmes, who was a Senator from Louisiana in the Confederate Congress at Richmond. From the New Orleans La.,* Picayune, *January 23, 1898.*]

An Evening with the Venerable Statesman and Jurist, Hon. Thomas J. Semmes

It was of that inner life of the Confederacy that he [Mr. Semmes] spoke most freely, those days of social life in Richmond, gay and brilliant as some olden court, and then varying in the scale of merriness as the end of the gamut was reached and Richmond found itself a doomed city.

"Yes, the social life in Richmond during the war was very beautiful, and characterized by that old-time grace and hospitality for which the South was famous. It was, indeed, the last chapter in the history of that olden life. We occupied a beautiful mansion known as the Cruikshanks house. It was one of the finest houses in Richmond, and almost a facsimile of that occupied by President Davis.

.   .   .   .

"Our home was the center of a most brilliant coterie. Alexander H. Stephens, of Georgia, Vice President of the Confederate States, was a bachelor, and asked to make his home with us. We also had Mr. Garland, afterwards a member of Mr. Cleveland's cabinet, and General Sparrow, my colleague. Of course, they did not want to accept my hospitality without paying board, and so we laughingly complied. My boarders during the last years of the war used to pay me about $900 a month, and we used to estimate the expenses of running our house at about $300,000 a year. Fancy that sum for household expenses, but you must remember that we were using Confederate money, and as Mrs. Semmes used to say, we would send a whole basketful of money to market in exchange for provisions. Our boarders in reality paid us   page 326/   about $100 a month, and towards the close of the war the money was not even valued at that. I was not a rich man, but my father-in-law was one of the wealthy men of the South, and he kept us liberally supplied with food."

"Yes, indeed," said Mrs. Semmes, "we used to get all manner of nice provisions and hampers from Montgomery, and never knew how they reached us so safely, for everything came to us contraband. Our table was always well supplied, and many were the brilliant dinners we gave. We often invited the Senators from the border States, for some of these fared very badly, indeed; they had to live in one room, and on corn and beans and bacon, and as their States were very much divided, supplies sent them by their constituents were cut off, and money, too. They had a hard time of it, but they stood nobly by the cause to the end. We had great times in the first years of the war, when our cause seemed so sure of success and our boys were fighting so bravely, but towards the end Mr. Stephens and Mr. Garland, General Sparrow and Mr. Semmes used to come home with weary hearts."

"But you were always bright and cheerful to the end," said Mr. Semmes. "It was wonderful, the courage of the Southern women during the war. In Richmond . . . the women kept up their social life. Parties and receptions and dances were given night after night; when our boys in gray passed through the capital, all the women went out to greet them, waving handkerchiefs and bidding them Godspeed. Receptions were given in their honor, and a perpetual round of gayety was kept up. The women did this to cheer on the soldier boys. Many a group of handsome officers danced the night away and went forth to fight on the morrow, and were buried in the evening shadows of the battle-field. There was General J. E. B. Stuart, the dashing cavalry officer, who, the night before he was killed, played in charades at the home of my sister, Mrs. Ives, wife of Colonel Ives, who was an officer on President Davis' staff. Mrs. Ives' home was a great center for the young folks. That night all the prettiest girls in Richmond were taking part in the charades, and some of the most brilliant officers in the army. There were present Mr. Davis, Mr. Stephens, Judah P. Benjamin, Secretary Mallory, Mrs. Mallory, — in fact, all the cabinet officers and their wives, the representatives in Congress, justices of the Supreme Court, etc., and General Stuart was the observed of all **page 327/** observers, as he gaily led the charades. . . ."

. . . .

Then [Mr. Semmes] spoke of Robert Lee: "General Lee was a frequent visitor at our house in Richmond; he was then, as he is today, the great ideal of Southern chivalry and truth. Great in defeat as he was in victory, the annals of the world's history bears no purer or greater name than that of Robert Lee." **page 328/**

. . . .

"Again events were hurrying forward, but not as at the beginning of the year 1861, when we all entered Richmond in such bright hopes. But the final catastrophe was delayed for a while yet. Colonel Dahlgren determined to make a raid upon Richmond, and when the news reached us, all there was to oppose him was a force of local soldiery and a battalion of department clerks. The members of the Congress shouldered guns and mounted guard around Richmond. But the small force of department clerks and unskilled soldiers were [sic] a match for Dahlgren and averted the plot he had formed to pour fire upon the devoted capital of the Confederacy. But we soldiers were hungry," continued Mr. Semmes. "I had had nothing to eat all day, and the heartiest meal I ever enjoyed was a piece of dry bread and a raw onion that I asked of an old market woman as she passed me where I was keeping guard. That was the best onion I ever ate in my life. Dark days were coming, however, for it had become apparent to all that the South must yield, not in bravery, but in superiority of numbers. In Virginia the supply of bread was exhausted, and little more could be expected until after the next wheat crop came in. Provisions of all kinds were enormously high."

"For instance," said Mrs. Semmes, "at our New Year's dinner in 1864, we had to pay $110 for the turkey to grace the feast. That was one of the last big dinners that we had at our house."

"It was not such a big dinner in point of courses," said Mr. Semmes, "for we were getting reduced now, and money was worth nothing and provisions were high. Nevertheless, it was a good substantial dinner: we had our Confederate turkey, and vegetables and game, and good bread, made at home, and nice dessert. . . . I shall never forget that New Year's dinner. We all tried to be gay, but our hearts were inwardly sad. There was the usual visiting, customary in those days on New Year's Day, but the old brilliancy and fire were fast ebbing away." **page 331/**

No. 135 The Richmond *Enquirer*, January 8, 1864, p. 1.

Weekly Levees

His Excellency Governor Smith, has resumed the fashion formerly in vogue, of giving weekly levees at the gubernatorial mansion. These social reunions are appointed to take place on every Friday night. The first one will take place tonight, when, doubtless, General Morgan [Brig. Gen. John H.] and other distinguished guests will be present.

No. 136 The Richmond *Enquirer*, January 22, 1864, p. 2.

Amusements for the Million

Suggestions are afloat for the establishment of a theatre in this city, for the amusement of the million and the pecuniary benefit of particular individuals. The notion is based upon the fact that "the present state of the drama" is, besides being decidedly imperfect, at a pretty low ebb, on the Richmond boards; and as the people, and especially the soldiers from the army will seek to amuse themselves by patronizing public entertainments, it is believed that their object can be more agreeably and completely secured by the establishment of a theatre, under the direction of a society, who will secure all the best dramatic talent in the Confederacy, pay liberally, and devote the surplus to the benefit of the army. This arrangement would unquestionably become popular; in fact so popular that the present theatre would in all probability, have to close up for want of patronage, provided the "society" did not slide into the tactics of the aforesaid present theatre, and end as it seems to have ended, in no theatre at all.

No. 137 John B. Jones, *A Rebel War Clerk's Diary*, New York, Old Hickory Bookshop, 1935, vol. II (2 vols.).

January 26, 1864: The prisoners on Belle Isle (8000) have had no meat for eleven days. The Secretary says the Commissary-General informs him that they fare as well as our armies, and so he refused the commissary (Capt. Warner) of the prisoners a permit to buy and bring to the city cattle he might be able to find. An outbreak of the prisoners is apprehended: and if they were to rise, it is feared some of the inhabitants of the city would join them, for they, too, have no meat — many of them — or bread either. They believe the famine is owing to the imbecility, or worse of the government. A riot would be a dangerous occurrence now: the city battalion would not fire *page 135/* on the people — and if they did the army might break up, and avenge their slaughtered kindred. It is a perilous time. *page 136/*

No. 138 Mrs. Roger A. Pryor, *Reminiscences of Peace and War*, New York, The Macmillan Company, 1905.

[On January 30, 1864, "Agnes" wrote from Richmond: —]

How can you be even dreaming of new cups and saucers? Mend your old ones, my dear, with white lead. That is what we are doing here; and when the cup is very much broken, the triangular, rectangular, and other 'angular lines' of white give it quite a Japanese effect. There is not a bit of China for sale in the Capital of the Confederacy. A forlorn little chipped set — twelve odd pieces — sold last week at auction for $200 — and as to hats and bonnets! We are washing the old ones and plaiting straw for the new. I'll send you a package of straw I gleaned and dyed for you last summer.

.   .   .   .   .   .

President and Mrs. Davis gave a large reception last week, and all the ladies looked positively gorgeous. Mrs. Davis is in mourning for her father. We should not expect suppers in these times, but we do have them! **page 263/**   Champagne is $350 a dozen, but we sometimes have champagne! The confectioners charge $15 for a cake, but we have cake! My flounced gray silk is behaving admirably, but I am afraid my Washington friends remember it as an old acquaintance. I never go out without meeting them. . . . I never could bear that Lord Lyons, with his red face and small eyes like ferrets'; and now we have reason to suppose that England would have recognized us but for his animosity against us. He says 'the Confederacy is on its last legs.' We have heard from dear old Dudley Mann; but of course *he* can do nothing for us in England, and he had as well come home and go with me to receptions. Mrs. Davis receives every Tuesday, and Mr. Mann is a better squire of dames than he is a diplomat. **page 264/**

No. 139 Mary Boykin Chesnut, *A Diary from Dixie,* Boston, Houghton Mifflin Company, 1949.

January 31, 1864: Mrs. Davis gave her "Luncheon to Ladies" on Saturday. Many more persons were there than at any of those luncheons which have gone before. We had gumbo, ducks and olives, *supreme de volaille,* chickens in jelly, oysters, lettuce salad, chocolate cream, jelly cake, claret cup, champagne, etc. **page 367/**

No. 140 The Richmond *Enquirer,* February 16, 1864, p. 2.

Sumptuous Repasts — Reception Days

We took occasion, some few days ago, to animadvert upon the gaiety of Richmond during the past winter and upon the new-fangled "reception days" which are attempted to be innovated upon the good old Virginia custom of social visiting. . . . We are no enemy of "innocent recreation," but only the decided opponent of untimely frivolity. . . .

We know there must be recreation even in the midst of mourning and sorrow, and it is the duty of all to take recreation, nor would we have persons nursing their sorrow — those who can laugh and dance at such a time should do so; but there is neither propriety nor necessity in accompanying the "innocent recreation" with a sumptuous repast which, while unnecessarily consuming provisions, actually robs others of the bread and meat required for their sustenance. It is not that people enjoy themselves that we condemn, but that in doing so, they consume the provisions required for the support of the army and the poor.

No. 141   *Daily Dispatch,* Richmond, Virginia, February 17, 1864, p. 2.

The Yankee Prisons

We understand that a good many of the Yankee prisoners are quite truculent and insulting, declaring that if they ever do get their freedom, they will slay, burn, and destroy in Richmond to their hearts' content. The immediate provocation of these dire menaces is that they do not always have sugar in their coffee. They need sweetening, no doubt, and if they received their deserts, would have no cause to complain of any deficiency in that particular. . . . We are not much alarmed at the threats of these fine fellows. They have been breathing blood and thunder against Richmond for the last three years, and it has all ended in the Libby [one of the largest tobacco ware-house prisons in Richmond]. That is the only "On to Richmond" which has been realized yet. We have no doubt that the Yankees will behave a great deal worse hereafter, if that be possible, than they have ever done before. But perhaps we shall behave worse also. There is great room for improvement in our mode of treating these invaders. . . . We are not always going to have our prisoners murdered by inches and our houses burned over our heads without some attempt at retaliation. In the meantime, the sooner the Yankees now here are removed further South, the better for all parties.

No. 142   The Richmond *Enquirer,* March 16, 1864, p. 2.

A Grand Reception

Richmond opened wide her arms on yesterday. For hours the hills of Rocketts bloomed with beauty, and the streets along the Navy Yard were alive with throngs of pleased, expectant, joyous-hearted people. The glittering muskets of a battalion shown in their midst, and the music of a band added to the attractions of the scene. At half past one o'clock, two steamers loaded with Confederate soldiers, just released from Northern prisons, after ten months of cruel captivity, appeared, coming slowly toward the wharf. — Cheers from the shore and cheers from the boats arose. As the boats touched the wharf, the prison-worn "heroes of many a fight" were seized upon by a thousand ladies or more, and welcomed with Virginia warmth and womanly enthusiasm. The military presented arms; the band did its best; the people cheered. — Everybody did something, or said or shouted something that evinced overflowing, irrepressible, indefinable gladness. The prisoners were then escorted uptown. The march was a triumph. They stopped in Capitol Square and were addressed from the monument by the President and the Governor. Five thousand persons were present. More cheering, music and welcome. Edibles and drinkables were circulated.

No. 143 Judith W. McGuire, *Diary of a Southern Refugee,* New York, E. J. Hale & Son, 1867.

March 20, 1864: Our Lent services in St. Paul's lecture-room, at seven o'clock in the morning, are delightful. The room is always crowded to overflowing — the old, the young, the grave, the gay, collect there soon after sunrise; also military officers in numbers. When General Lee is in town, as he is now, he is never absent, and, always one of the most devout worshippers. Within a few days I have seen General Whiting there; also Generals Ransom, Pegram, and **page 255/** others. Starred officers of all grades, colonels, majors, etc., together with many others belonging to the rank and file; and civilians of every degree. It is delightful to see them, all bending together before high Heaven, imploring the help which we so much need.

The Transportation Office is just opposite to us, where crowds of furloughed soldiers, returning to their commands, are constantly standing waiting for transportation. As I pass them . . . I always stop to have a cheerful word with them. Yesterday morning I said to them: "Gentlemen, whom do you suppose I have seen this morning?" In answer to their inquiring looks, I said: "General Lee." "General Lee," they exclaimed: "I did not know he was in town; God bless him!" and they looked excited, as if they were about to burst forth with "Hurrah for General Lee!" "And where do you suppose I saw him so early?" "Where, Madam — where?" "At prayer meeting, down upon his knees, praying for you and for the country." In an instant they seemed subdued; tears started to the eyes of many of those hardy, sun-burnt veterans. Some were utterly silent, while others exclaimed with various ejaculations, "God bless him!" "God bless his dear old soul!" etc. As I walked away some followed me to know where he was to be seen. One had never seen him at all, and wanted to see him "monstrous bad;" others had seen him often, but wanted to see him in town, "just to look at him." . . . It is delightful **page 256/** to see how they reverence him, and almost as much for his goodness as for his greatness. **page 257/**

No. 144 John B. Jones, *A Rebel War Clerk's Diary,* New York, Old Hickory Bookshop, 1935, vol. II (2 vols.).

March 21, 1864: Yesterday another thousand prisoners were brought up by the flag of truce boat. A large company of both sexes welcomed them in the Capitol Square, whither some baskets of food were sent by those who had some patriotism with their abundance. The President made them a comforting speech, alluding to their toils, bravery **page 174/** and sufferings in captivity; and promised them, after a brief respite, that they should be in the field again.

The following conversation took place yesterday between the President and some young ladies of his acquaintance, with whom he promenaded:

Miss. — Do you think they will like to return to the field?

President. — It may seem hard; but even those boys (pointing to some youths around the monument twelve or fourteen years old) will have their trial.

Miss. — But how shall the army be fed?

President. — I don't see why rats, if fat, are not as good as squirrels. Our men *did* eat mule meat at Vicksburg; but it would be an expensive luxury now.

After this the President fell into a grave mood, and some remarks about recognition caused him to say twice — "We have no friends abroad!"   page 175/

No. 145 The Richmond *Enquirer,* March 23, 1864, p. 1.

Shakespeare's Birthday

The 23rd of April next will be celebrated abroad as the third centennial anniversary of the birthday of Shakespeare, . . . Richmond, in better times, would desire no fairer opportunity than this centennial anniversary to do homage to the genius of the "Sweet Swan of Avon." What smoking venison and sparkling wines, what mugs of foaming ale, and dishes of rich meats and delicious pastries would be offered up to the ghost of the valiant Sir John Falstaff. What wit would flow in memory of the grave-digger, and what eloquence burst out in remembrance of Lear, in sympathy with Hamlet, and in love for Juliet. But "grim-visaged war" has unfortunately stepped in and spoiled our fun. Our supply of roast beef is limited; our foaming ale is too inexpressibly thin to do justice to the event; our whiskey would disgrace even the "miserable sack" of Sir John; and then, worst of all dramatically speaking, Richmond is inadequate to the occasion. An attempt to make a display would be a failure. Peace, therefore, we trust, will be accorded to the ashes of Shakespeare.

No. 146 Mary Boykin Chesnut, *A Diary from Dixie,* Boston, Houghton Mifflin Company, 1949.

March 24, 1864: Yesterday we went to the Capitol grounds to see our returned prisoners. . . . The President joined us. We walked slowly up and down until Jeff Davis was called upon to speak to the prisoners. Then I stood, almost touching the bayonets, where he left me. I looked straight into the prisoners' faces. Poor fellows! They cheered with all their might, and I wept for sympathy. Their enthusiasm moved me deeply. Oh, these men were so forlorn, so dried up, so shrunken. There was a strange look in the eyes of some; others were so restless and wild looking; others again had placidly vacant faces, as if they had been dead to the world for years. A poor woman was too much for me. She was hunting for her son. He had been expected back with this batch of prisoners. She said he was taken prisoner at Gettysburg. She kept going in and out among them with a basket of provisions she had brought for him to eat. It was too pitiful. She was   page 397/ utterly unconscious of the crowd. The anxious dread, expectation, hurry and hope which led her on showed in her face.   page 398/

No. 147   The Richmond *Enquirer*, March 24, 1864, p. 1.

Feeding the Poor

The city supply depot continues to furnish large numbers of the needy with the necessaries of life. The officers of the depot say that every applicant has been supplied, and the distribution continues with regularity and satisfaction. If any poor person has been without food or fuel any day during the past winter or the present spring, they are unknown to the distributors. . . .

No. 148   The Richmond *Enquirer*, April 7, 1864, p. 1.

[This is one of several similar proclamations made by the President throughout the course of the war.]

Proclamation by the President of the Confederate States of America

. . . I, Jefferson Davis, President of the Confederate States of America, do issue this my proclamation, calling upon the people of the said states, in conformity with the desire expressed by their representatives, to set apart Friday, the 8th day of April, as a day of Humiliation, Fasting, and Prayer, and I do hereby invite them on that day to repair to their several places of public worship and beseech Almighty God "to preside over our public counsels, and to inspire our armies and leaders with wisdom, courage and perseverance, and so to manifest Himself in the greatness of his goodness, and in the majesty of His power, that we may secure the blessings of an honorable peace, and of free government; and that we, as a people, may ascribe all to the Honor and Glory of His name."

Given under my hand and the seal of the Confederate States of America, at the city of Richmond, on this 12th day of March, in the year of Our Lord one thousand eight hundred and sixty-four.

JEFFERSON DAVIS

By the President:
  J. P. Benjamin
      Secretary of State

No. 149 The Richmond *Enquirer*, April 15, 1864, p. 3.

A Neat Present for General Lee

We saw on yesterday a set of wreaths and cuffs for a general's uniform coat, and wreaths for a field jacket, made by the Misses Semon, 98 Main Street, and designed as a present for General Lee. The embroidery is in pure gold thread and executed with admirable skill. Accurately appreciating the General's taste, nothing gaudy has been attempted.

No. 150 The Richmond *Enquirer*, April 26, 1864, p. 1.

The Cuffs and Collar Wreaths for General Lee

The elegant cuffs and collar wreaths, embroidered by the Misses Semon, of this city, for General Robert E. Lee, have reached their destination, and are acknowledged by their distinguished recipient as follows:

Orange Court House, April 18, 1864
Misses Semon: — I have received the collar wreaths, sleeve cuffs, &c, which you have embroidered for me. They are beautifully executed. I can only return my grateful thanks for your kindness and for the pains and labor they have cost you. For the safety of your home in Richmond, you are indebted to a Munificent Providence, and to the brave army of Northern Virginia, which alone are entitled to your thanks and gratitude.

With sentiments of great respect,
Your obedient servant,
R. E. Lee

No. 151 Varina Howell Davis, *Jefferson Davis*, New York, Belford Company, 1890, vol. II (2 vols.).

One noteworthy example of the self-sacrifice of our soldiers is remembered with especial pride. On June 15 and 17, 1864, the women and children of Richmond had been suffering for food, and the Thirtieth Virginia sent them one day's rations of flour, pork, bacon and veal, not from their abundance, but by going without the day's rations themselves. "Yet," said a journal of that time, "despatches from General Lee show that nearly every regiment in his army has re-enlisted for the war."

On April 30th, when we were threatened on every side, and encompassed so perfectly that we could only hope by a miracle to overcome our foes, Mr. Davis's health declined from loss of sleep so that he forgot to eat, and I resumed the practice of carrying him something at one o'clock. I left my children quite well, playing in my room, and had just uncovered my basket in his office, when a servant came for me. The most beautiful and brightest   **page 496/** of my children, Joseph Emory, had, in play, climbed over the connecting angle of a bannister and fallen to the brick pavement below. He died a few minutes after we reached his side. This child was Mr. Davis's hope, and greatest joy in life. At intervals, he ejaculated, "Not mine, oh, Lord, but Thine." A courier came with a despatch. He took it, held it open for some moments, and looked at me fixedly, saying, "Did you tell me what was in it?" I saw his mind was momentarily paralyzed by the blow, but at last he tried to write an answer, and then called out, in a heart-broken tone, "I must have this day with my little child." Somebody took the despatch to General Cooper and left us alone with our dead.   **page 497/**

No. 152 Constance Cary Harrison, *Recollections, Grave and Gay*, New York, Charles Scribner's Sons, 1912.

No feeling heart in Richmond failed to yield tender sympathy to the President's family in the calamity that befell them when little, merry, happy "Joe," petted by all visitors to the Executive Mansion — he who, when his father was in the act of receiving official visitors, once pushed his way into the study and, clad only in an abbreviated night-gown, insisting upon saying his evening prayer at the President's knee — fell from the porch in   **page 181/** the rear of their dwelling and was picked up dead on the brick pavement underneath. From Burton Harrison, upon whom devolved all arrangements in behalf of the stricken parents, we heard a pitiful tale of the mother's passionate grief and the terrible self-control of the President, who, shutting himself in his own room, had walked the floor without ceasing all of the first night. To the bier of the little lad, it seemed that every child in Richmond brought flowers and green leaves.   **page 182/**

No. 153 *Official Records of the Union and Confederate Armies*, series II, volume VII, Washington, Government Printing Office, 1899.

Office Commissary-General of Prisoners,
Washington, D.C., May 3, 1864.
Hon. E. M. Stanton, Secretary of War, Washington, D.C.:
Sir: I have the honor to report that, pursuant to your instructions of the 2d instant, I proceeded yesterday morning to Annapolis, with a view to see that the

paroled prisoners about to arrive there from Richmond were properly received and cared for. **page 110/**

.   .   .   .   .   .

The enlisted men who had endured so many privations at Belle Isle and other places were, with few exceptions, in a very sad plight, mentally and physically, having for months been exposed to all the changes of the weather with no other protection than a very insufficient supply of worthless tents, and with an allowance of food scarcely sufficient to prevent starvation, even if of wholesome quality, but as it was made of coarsely ground corn, including the husks, and probably at times the cobs, if it did not kill by starvation it was sure to do it by the disease it created. Some of these poor fellows were wasted to mere skeletons and had scarcely life enough remaining to appreciate that they were now in the hands of their friends, and among them all there were few who had not become too much broken down and dispirited by their many privations to be able to realize the happy prospect of relief from their sufferings which was before them. With rare exceptions, every face was sad with care and hunger; there was no brightening of the countenance or lighting up of the eye to indicate a thought of anything beyond a painful sense of prostration of mind and body. Many faces showed that there was scarcely a ray of intelligence left.

.   .   .   .   .   .

That our soldiers when in the hands of the rebels are starved to death cannot be denied. Every return of the flag-of-truce boat from City Point brings too many living and dying witnesses to admit of a doubt of this terrible fact. I am informed that the authorities at Richmond admit the fact, but excuse it on the plea that they give the prisoners the same ration they give their own men. But can this be so? Can an army keep the field and be active and efficient on the same fare that kills prisoners of war at a frightful percentage? I think not, no man can believe it, and while a practice so shocking to humanity is persisted in by the rebel authorities I would very respectfully urge that retaliatory measures be at once instituted by subjecting the officers we now hold as prisoners of war to a similar treatment. **page 111/**

.   .   .   .   .   .

I have the honor to be, very respectfully, your obedient servant,

W. HOFFMAN

Colonel Third Infantry and Commissary-General of Prisoners.

No. 154   *Official Records of the Union and Confederate Armies,* series II, volume VII, Washington, Government Printing Office, 1899.

War Department, Washington City, May 4, 1864.

Hon. B. F. Wade,

    Chairman of Joint Committee on Conduct of the War:

    Sir: I have the honor to submit to you a report made to this Department by Colonel Hoffman, Commissary-General of Prisoners, in regard to the condition of Union soldiers who have, until within a few days, been prisoners of war at Richmond, and would respectfully request that your committee immediately proceed to Annapolis to take testimony there and examine with their own eyes the condition of those who have been returned from rebel captivity. The enormity of crime committed by the rebels toward our prisoners for the last several months is not known or realized by our people, and cannot but fill with horror the civilized world when the facts are fully revealed. There appears to have been a deliberate system of savage and barbarous treatment and starvation, the result of which will be that few, if any, of the prisoners that have been in their hands during the past winter will ever again be in a condition to render any service or even to enjoy life. page 110/

Your obedient servant,

Edward M. Stanton,
Secretary of War.

No. 155 Mary Boykin Chesnut, *A Diary from Dixie,* Boston, Houghton Mifflin Company, 1949.

May 8, 1864: John Witherspoon [friend of the Chesnuts'] says the President did wrong when he did not arrest Joe Johnston before Seven Pines, when Johnston was in full retreat, apparently ready to abandon Richmond, with Virginia crying: "If you cannot defend our Capital, we will." . . . "Yes," says John Witherspoon, growing red with suppressed fury, "if the President had sent him out of the Confederacy, sent him to Sherman and McClellan who admire him so much, it would have saved us! Joe Johnston's disaffection with our President and our policy has acted like a dry rot in our armies. It has served as an excuse for all selfishness, all stay-at-home-a-tiveness, all languid patriotism." After this, for him, long speech he asked: "Did you ever see Joe Johnston and the President together?"

"No, but I did see Mr. and Mrs. Davis and Mrs. Johnston at the Spotswood, and I firmly believe if he could have promoted Joe Johnston consistently with his duty to his country he would have done so. I do   page 410/   not know how the split began. They were as intimate and as affectionate as people could be when I left them."

"I'll tell you," said John Witherspoon. "He made Joe Johnston a dissatisfied general when he refused to make him Number One in the Confederate Army. The breach had been ruinous!"

May 27, 1864: I hate these constant attacks on Jeff Davis. Old hard-common-sense Lincoln, the essence of a cute Yankee, says "don't swap horses crossing a stream." In battering down our administration, these people are destroying our last hope of success.   page 411/

No. 156 *Daily Richmond Examiner,* May 14, 1864, p. 2.

Burial of Major General J. E. B. Stuart, Flower of Cavaliers

The funeral services, preliminary to the consignment to the grave of the remains of General Stuart, were conducted yesterday afternoon in St. James' Episcopal Church, corner of Marshall and Fifth Streets, Rev. Dr. Peterkin, rector. The cortege reached the church about five o'clock, without music or military escort, the Public Guard being absent on duty. The church was already crowded with citizens. The metallic case, containing the corpse, was borne into the church and up into the center aisle to the altar, the organ pealing a solemn funeral dirge and anthem by the choir.

Among the congregation appeared President Davis, General Bragg, General Ransom, and other civil and military officials in Richmond. A portion of the funeral services, according to the Episcopal Church, was read by Rev. Dr. Peterkin, assisted by other ministers, concluding with singing and prayer.

The body was then borne forth to the hearse in waiting, decorated with black plumes and drawn by four white horses. . . . From the church the cortege moved to Hollywood Cemetery, where the remains were deposited in a vault, the concluding portion of the affecting service read by Rev. Dr. Minnegerode [sic], of St. Paul's Church, and all that was mortal of the dead hero was shut in from the gaze of men.

No. 157 Phoebe Yates Pember, *A Southern Woman's Story,* New York, G. W. Carleton and Co., 1879.

The horrors that attended, in past times, the bombardment of a city, were experienced in a great degree in Richmond during the fighting around us. The close proximity to the scenes of strife, the din of battle, the bursting of shells, the fresh wounds of the men hourly brought in were daily occurrences. Walking through the streets during this time, after the duties of the hospital   page 127/ were over, when night had well advanced, the pavement around the railroad depot would be crowded with wounded men just brought in, and laid there waiting for conveyance to the receiving hospitals. Some on stretchers, others on the bare bricks, or laid on a thin blanket, suffering from wounds hastily wrapped around with strips of coarse, unbleached, galling bandages of homespun cotton, on which the blood had congealed and stiffened until every crease cut like a knife. Women passing accidentally, like myself, would put down their basket or their bundle, and ringing at the bell of neighboring homes, ask for basin and soap, warm water, and a few soft rags, and going from sufferer to sufferer, try to alleviate with what skill they possessed, the pain of fresh wounds, change the uneasy posture, and allay the thirst.

Others would pause and look on, till the labor appearing to require no particular talent, they too would follow the example set them, and occasionally asking a word of advice, do their duty carefully and willingly. Idle boys would get a pine-knot or tallow-dip, and stand quietly and curiously as torch-bearers, till the scene, with **page 128/** its gathering accessories formed a strange picture, not easily forgotten. Persons driving in different vehicles would alight, sometimes in evening dress, and choosing the wounded most in need of surgical aid, put them in their places, and send them to their destination, continuing their way on foot. There was little conversation carried on, no necessity for introductions, and no names ever asked or given. **page 129/**

No. 158 The Richmond *Enquirer,* May 20, 1864, p. 1.

Prices

The cost of all articles of prime necessity has increased to an alarming extent during the past week. Pious people are hoping that those who have raised prices till they are nearly out of sight will go up after the objects of their solicitude and stay after they get up. What will people say after this war when they remember that flour and rice has [sic] been sold at $2.50 per pound; butter at $14 and $20; and eggs at $10.00 per dozen. The stoppage of communications with the city may have had something to do with the high prices, but we suggest that they are more owing to the natural disposition of holders to get all they can out of the people.

No. 159 The Richmond *Enquirer,* June 2, 1864, p. 2.

. . . while everyday the booming of death-dealing ordnance peals on the ears of the citizens of this metropolis, what a singular aspect does the city afford? Utterly regardless of the fact that within a few miles of their homes a foe, fiercer and more barbarous than ever the cohorts of Bonaparte were, the citizens of Richmond pursue their daily avocations with the calmness of the palmiest days of peace. On the streets the little children stop from their play to listen to the sullen sound of the distant gun. As evening advances, that great resort of all classes, Capitol Square, is thronged with laughing girls, indulging in the refreshing coolness after the heat of the day, careless of that foe, whose triumph would subject them to a fate far worse than the destruction of that vital spark which occasions their vivacity and light-heartedness. As in days of old, neighbors and friends pass away the summer evenings in social visits of friendly tea parties. And in the midst of all, the Congress of the nation is coolly deliberating upon the prospects and affairs of the infant Confederacy, whilst the thunder of its orators is echoed from the lines of Lee's indomitable army. Such a spectacle was rarely, if ever witnessed since the foundation of the world.

No. 160 John B. Jones, *A Rebel War Clerk's Diary*, New York, Old Hickory Bookshop, 1935, vol. II (2 vols.).

August 24, 1864: I wrote a letter to the President today, urging the necessity of preventing the transportation of any supplies on the railroads except for distribution at cost, and thus exterminating the speculators. The poor must be fed and protected, if they be relied upon to defend the country. The rich bribe the conscription officers, and keep out of the ranks, invest their Confederate money and bonds in real estate, and would be the first to submit to the United States Government; and the poor whom they oppress, are in danger of demoralization from suffering and disgust, and might also embrace reunion rather than a prolongation of such miseries as they have so long experienced. The patriotism of 1861 must be revived, or independence cannot be achieved. . . . The surest plan is to break up speculation, and put the rich as well as the poor in the army. We must *deserve* independence, else we shall not get it. There must be no partiality, and especially in favor of the rich. **page 271/**

No. 161 Mrs. Roger A. Pryor, *Reminiscences of Peace and War,* New York, The Macmillan Company, 1905.

["Agnes" wrote from Richmond, August 26, 1864: —]

You dear, obstinate little woman! What did I tell you? I implored you to get away while you could, and now you are waiting placidly for General Grant to blow you up. That awful crater! Do the officers around you consider it honorable warfare to dig and mine under a man and blow him up while he is asleep — before he has time to get his musket? I always thought an open field and a fair fight, with the enemy in front at equal chances,   **page 292/**   was the American idea of honest, manly warfare. To my mind this is the most awful thing that could be imagined. There is a strong feeling among the people I meet that the hour has come when we should consider the lives of the few men left to us. Why let the enemy wipe us off the face of the earth? Should this feeling grow, nothing but a great victory can stop it. Don't you remember what Mr. Hunter said to us in Washington? 'You may sooner check with your bare hand the torrent of Niagara than stop this tidal wave of secession.' I am for a tidal wave of peace — and I am not alone. Meanwhile we are slowly starving to death. Here, in Richmond, if we can afford to give $11 for a pound of bacon, $10 for a small dish of green corn, and $10 for a watermelon, we can have a dinner of three courses for four persons. Hampton's cavalry passed through town last week, amid great excitement. Every man as he trotted by was cutting and eating a watermelon, and throwing the rinds on the heads of the little negro boys who followed in crowds on either side of the street. You wouldn't have dreamed of war — such shouting and laughing from everybody. The contrasts we constantly see look like insanity in our people. The President likes to call attention to the fact that we have no beggars on our streets, as evidence that things are not yet desperate with us. He forgets our bread riot which occurred such a little while ago. That pale, thin woman with the wan smile haunts me. Ah! these are the people who suffer the consequences of all that talk about slavery in the territories you and I used to hear in the House and Senate Chamber. Somebody, somewhere is mighty to blame for all this business, but it isn't you nor I, nor yet the women who did not really deserve to have Governor Letcher send the Mayor to read the Riot Act to them. They were only hungry, and so a thousand of them loaded some carts with bread for their children. You are not to page 293/ suppose I am heartless because I run on in this irrelevant fashion. The truth is, I am so shocked and disturbed I am hysterical. It is all so awful. page 294/

Your scared to death
"Agnes"

No. 162   Constance Cary Harrison, *Recollections, Grave and Gay*, New York, Charles Scribner's Sons, 1912.

To multiply instances of our work among the suffering that long, long summer would be monotonous. [The summer of 1864, during which, among others, were fought the bloody battles of The Wilderness, Spottsylvania Court House, Yellow Tavern, Cold Harbor.] I depict it as an example of a life led by hundreds of women of the South — women who had mostly come out of beautiful and luxurious homes. My mother, previously a volunteer, was now a paid servant of government, and, of what she received, spent the greater part in amplifying the conveniences and supplies of her diet kitchen. We were then in straits for everything considered indispensable in the outfit of modern hospitals. Our surgeons, working with pure devotion, were at their wits' ends to renew needful appliances. Without going into painful detail, I can say that our experience was continually shocking and distressing, as were the burials of our dead in a field by Hollywood, six or seven coffins dropped into a yawning pit, and hurriedly covered in, all that a grateful country could render page 188/ in return for precious lives. All told, that Camp Winder [a hospital] episode was the most ghastly I ever knew. If we had possessed enough of any one hospital requisite it would have been less grim!   page 189/

No. 163   Phoebe Yates Pember, *A Southern Woman's Story*, New York, G. W. Carleton and Co., 1879.

The summer of 1864 passed, and early in September our hearts were gladdened by the tidings that the exchange of prisoners was to be renewed. The sick and the wounded of our hospital [the author was a matron in Chimborazo Hospital] (but few in number just then), were transferred to other quarters, and the wards put in order to receive our men from Northern prisons.

Can any pencil do justice to those squalid pictures of famine and desolation? Those gaunt, lank skeletons with the dried yellow flesh clinging to bones enlarged by **page 120/** dampness and exposure. Those pale, bluish lips and feverish eyes, glittering and weird when contrasted with the famine-stricken faces; — that flitting, piteous, scared smile which greeted their fellow creatures, all will live forever before the mental vision that then witnessed it.

Living and dead were taken from the flag of truce boat, not distinguishable save from the difference of care exercised in moving them. The Federal prisoners we had released were in many instances in a like state, but our ports had been blockaded, our harvests burned, our cattle stolen, our country wasted. Even had we the desire to succor, where could the wherewithall be found? But the foe, — the ports of the world were open to him. He could have fed his prisoners upon milk and honey, and not have missed either. When we review the past, it would seem that Christianity was but a name — that the Atonement had failed, and Christ had lived and died in vain. . . . **page 121/**

No. 164 John B. Jones, *A Rebel War Clerk's Diary*, New York, Old Hickory Bookshop, 1935, vol. II (2 vols.).

September 21, 1864: I look for other and more disastrous defeats, unless the speculators are demolished, and the wealthy class put in the ranks. Many of the privates in our army are fast becoming what is termed machine soldiers, and will ere long cease to fight well — having nothing to fight for. Alas! the chivalry have fallen! The lagging land proprietors and slaveowners (as the Yankees shrewdly predicted) want to be captains, etc. or speculators. The poor will not long fight for their oppressors, the money-changers, extortioners, etc., whose bribes keep them out of the service. **page 288/**

No. 165 John B. Jones, *A Rebel War Clerk's Diary*, New York, Old Hickory Bookshop, 1935, vol. II (2 vols.).

September 22, 1864: "When the cat's away, the mice will play," is an old saying, and a true one. I saw a note of invitation today from Secretary Mallory to Secretary Seddon, inviting him to his house at 5 P.M. to partake of "pea-soup" with Secretary Trenholm. His "pea-soup" will be oysters and champagne, and every other delicacy relished by epicures. Mr. Mallory's red face, and his plethoric body, indicate the highest living; and his party will enjoy the dinner while so many of our brave men are languishing with wounds, or pining in a cruel captivity. Nay, they may feast, possibly, while the very pillars of the government are crumbling under the blows of the enemy. **page 290/**

No. 166 *Daily Richmond Examiner,* September 24, 1864, p. 2.

The final struggle for the possession of Richmond and of Virginia is now near. This war draws to a close. If Richmond is held by the South till the first of November it will be ours forever more; for the North will never throw another huge army into the abyss where so many lie; and the war will conclude, beyond a doubt, with the independence of the Southern States.

No. 167 Richmond *Daily Whig,* October 5, 1864, p. 1.

That the present condition of affairs, compared with that of any previous year at the same season, at least since 1861, is greatly in our favor, we think can hardly be denied.

. . . . . .

. . . That General Lee can keep Grant out of Richmond from this time until doomsday, if he should be tempted to keep up the trial so long, we are as confident as we can be of anything whatever.

No. 168 *Daily Richmond Examiner,* October 7, 1864, p. 2.

One month of spirit and energy now, and the campaign is over, and the war is over. We do not mean that if the year's campaign end favorably for us, McClellan will be elected as Yankee President. That may come, or may not come; but no part of our chance for an honorable peace and independence rests upon that. Let who will be Yankee President, with the failure of Grant and Sherman this year, the war ends. And with Sherman's army already isolated and cut off in Georgia, and Grant unable either to take or besiege Richmond, we have only to make one month's exertion in improving our advantages, and then it may safely be said that the fourth year's campaign, and with it the war itself, is one gigantic failure.

No. 169 Sallie A. Brock Putnam, *Richmond During the War,* New York, G. W. Carleton and Company, 1867.

. . . It was no unusual thing to have presented at our doors a basket in the hands of a negro servant who sold on commission articles disposed of by the neces-

sitous to obtain food. Handsome dresses, patterns of unmade goods, purchased per-
hap before the commencement or in the beginning of the war, a piece of silver,
or sets of jewelry, accompanied by a note, anonymously sent, attested the poverty and
noble pride of some woman who doubtless wore a cheerful face, and when asked if
she desired peace, would reply, "Only with liberty." In the stores of our jewelers
were frequently seen diamonds and pearls, watches and valuable plates for sale,
placed there by some unfortunate, who disposed of these articles of former wealth,
luxury, and taste, to procure necessary articles of food and raiment. On the shelves
of booksellers valuable libraries were placed, to be disposed of for the same purpose,
and sometimes richly bound annuals, tasteful articles of vertu, and cherished memen-
toes of former friendships, all whispering a mute but eloquent story of want, privation
and suffering.   page 253/

No. 170 Myrta Lockett Avary, *A Virginia Girl in the Civil War 1861-1865,* New
York, D. Appleton and Company, 1903.

We all bought coal in common. Mother's, mine, and Delia's [a friend from
Petersburg] portion of the coal was a ton, and we had to keep it in our room —
there was no other place to store it. We had a box in our room which held a ton,
and the coal was brought up-stairs and dumped into that box. I can see those
darkies now, puffing and blowing, as they brought that coal up those many steps.
And how we had to scuffle around to pay them! For some jobs we paid in trade —
only we had very little to trade off. How that room held all its contents, I can't
make out. Dan [her husband] sent me provisions by the quantity when he could get
any and get them through to me. He would send a bag of potatoes or peas, and he
never sent less than a firkin of butter — delicious butter from Orange County. The
bags of peas, rice, and potatoes were disposed around the room, and around the
hearth were arranged our pots, pans, kettles, and cooking utensils generally. When
we bought wood that was put under the beds. In addition to all our useful and
ornamental articles we had our three   page 352/   selves and our trunks; such
clothing as we possessed had to be hung up for better keeping — and this was a
time when it behooved us to cherish clothes tenderly. Then there was our laundrying,
which was done in that room by ourselves.

And we had company! Certainly we seemed to have demonstrated the truth of
the adage, "Ole Virginny never tire." We had company, and we had company to eat
with us, and enjoyed it.   page 353/

No. 171 Constance Cary Harrison, *Recollections, Grave and Gay,* New York,
Charles Scribner's Sons, 1912.

. . . Now was instituted the "Starvation Club," of which, as one of the original
founders, I can speak with authority. It was agreed between a number of young
women that a place for our soldier visitors to meet with us for dancing and chat, once

a week, would be a desirable variation upon evening calls in private homes. The hostesses who successively offered their drawing-rooms were among the leaders in society. It was also decided that we should permit no one to infringe the rule of suppressing all refreshment, save the amber-hued water from the classic James. We began by having piano music for the dances, but the male members of the club made up between them a subscription providing a small but good orchestra. Before our first meeting, a committee of girls waited on General Lee to ask his sanction, with the result to the spokeswoman, who had ended with: "If you say no, general, we won't dance a single step!" "Why, of course, my dear child. My boys need to be heartened when they get their furloughs. Go on, look your prettiest, and be just as nice to them as ever you can be!"

We even had cotillions, to which everybody contributed favors. The gatherings were the jolliest imaginable. We had constant demands to admit new members, and all foreigners and general officers who visited Richmond were presented to our club, as a means of viewing the best society of the South.   **page 150/**

No. 172 Sallie A. Brock Putnam, *Richmond During the War*, New York, G. W. Carleton and Company, 1867.

Our social gatherings during this winter [1864-65] were much more frequent than those of the two previous winters. They were, however, distinguished for their extreme simplicity. There existed in Richmond, among the young people of the best class of society, a club known as the "Starvation Club," which weekly, or semi-weekly, assembled at different houses in the city for social enjoyment. Money was contributed amongst them in payment for the music required for dancing; but all refreshments were strictly forbidden, and the only expense to the generous host whose house might be impressed for the novel reception of the "Starvation Club," was an extra fire in the rear parlor, then not in every-day use, from the scarcity and high price of fuel. These entertainments were varied occasionally by the performance of plays and tableaux vivants, in which considerable talent was exhibited in the histrionic art by some of the quickly created actors and actresses. This introduction of plays and tableaux added an exquisitely charming variety to the winter's social enjoyment in the rebel capital.   **page 270/**

No. 173 Douglas Southall Freeman, *R. E. Lee*, New York, Charles Scribner's Sons, 1934-35, vol. III (4 vols.).

The capital was more crowded than ever, dejected and negligently dilapidated. Sometimes, from the sad seniors, Lee would turn away to the children. "I don't want to see you," he would   **page 527/**   say half in jest and half in reproof, "you are too gloomy and despondent; where is ——?" and he would name the little girl of the family. The young belles of the town were much in doubt whether it was proper to have dances at so dark a time, and a committee of them asked his advice, with the assurance that if he disapproved, they would not dance a single step. "Why, of course, my dear child," he answered. "My boys need to be heartened up when they get their furloughs. Go on, look your prettiest, and be just as nice to them as ever you can be!" page 528/

No. 174 T. C. DeLeon, *Four Years in Rebel Capitals,* Mobile, Alabama, The Gossip Printing Company, 1890.

But of all the bright coteries in Richmond society — its very page 309/ arcanum of wit, brilliance and culture — rise to memory that wholly unique set, that came somehow to be called "the Mosaic Club." Organization it was none; only a clique of men and women — married as well as single — that comprised the best intellects and prettiest accomplishments of the Capital. Many of the ladies were . . . "easy goers;" ever tolerant, genial and genuine at the *symposia* of the Mosaics, as they showed behind the *chevaux-de-frise* of knitting needles elsewhere. Some of them have since graced happy and luxurious homes; some have struggled with poverty and sorrow as only true womanhood may struggle; some have fought out the battle of life, sleeping now at rest forever. But one and all then faced their duty — sad, bitter, uncongenial as it might be — with loyalty and tender truth; one and all were strong enough to put by somber things, when meet to do so, and enjoy to the full the better pleasures society might offer.

And the men one met wore wreaths upon their collars often; quite as likely *chevrons* of "the men" upon their sleeves. Cabinet ministers, poets, statesmen, artists, and clergymen even were admitted to the "Mosaics;" the only "Open sesame!" to which its doors fell wide being that patent of nobility stamped by brain and worth alone.

Without organization, without officers; grown of itself and meeting as chance, or winter inactivity along army lines dictated — the Mosaic Club had no habitat. Collecting in one hospitable parlor, or another — as good fortune happened to provide better material for the delighting "muffin-match," or the entrancing "waffle-worry," as these festal procedures were sometimes called — the intimates who chanced in town were bidden; or, hearing of it, came to the feast of waffles and the flow of coffee — real coffee! without bids. They were ever welcome and knew it; and they were likewise sure of something even better than muffins, or coffee, to society-hungry men from the camps. And once gathered, the serious business of "teaing" over, the fun of the evening began.

The unwritten rule — indeed, the only rule — was the "forfeit essay," a game productive of so much that was novel and brilliant, that no later invention of peace-times has equaled it. At each meeting two hats would be handed round, all drawing a question from one, a word from the other; question and word to be connected in either a song, poem, essay, or tale for the next meeting. Then page 310/ after the drawing for forfeits, came the result of the last lottery of brain; interspersed with music by the best performers and singers of the city; with jest and seriously-brilliant talk, until the wee sma' hours, indeed. page 311/

No. 175 Southern Historical Society Papers, Richmond, Virginia, 1876-1943, vol. XIX (49 vols.).

[From the *Cosmopolitan,* December, 1891]

Social Life in Richmond During the War

EDWARD M. ALFRIEND

For many months after the beginning of the war between the states Richmond was an extremely gay, bright, and happy city. Except that its streets were filled with handsomely-attired officers and that troops constantly passed through it, there was nothing to indicate the horrors and sorrows of war, or the fearful deprivations that subsequently befell it.

. . . .

And yet, during the entire war, Richmond had happy phases to its social life. Entertainments were given very freely and very liberally the first year of the war, and at them wine and suppers were generously furnished, but as the war progressed all this was of necessity given up, and we had instead what were called "starvation parties."

The young ladies of the city, accompanied by their male escorts (generally Confederate officers on leave) would assemble at a fashionable residence that before the war had been the abode of wealth, and have music and plenty of dancing, but not a morsel of food or a drop of drink was seen. And this form of entertainment became the popular and universal one in Richmond. . . . **page 380/**

. . . often on the occasion of these starvation parties some young southern girl would appear in an old gown belonging to her mother or grandmother, or possibly a still more remote ancestor, and the effect of this antique garment was very peculiar; but no matter what was worn, no matter how peculiarly any one might be attired, no matter how bad the music, no matter how limited the host's or hostesses's ability to entertain, everybody laughed, danced, and was happy although the reports of the cannon often boomed in their ears, and all deprivation, all deficiencies were looked on as a sacrifice to the southern cause. **page 381/**

. . . .

On one occasion when I was attending a starvation party in Richmond the dancing was at its height and everybody was bright and happy, when the hostess, who was a widow, was suddenly called out of the room. A hush fell on everything, the dancing stopped, and everyone became sad, all having a premonition in those troublous times that something fearful had happened. We were soon told that her son had been killed late that evening in a skirmish in front of Richmond, a few miles from his home. **page 382/**

. . . .

Private theatricals were also a form of amusements during the war. I saw several of them. The first I witnessed, however, was a performance of Sheridan's comedy, *The Rivals,* in which that brilliant lady Mrs. Senator Clay, of Alabama, played Mrs. Malaprop. Her rendition of the part was one of the best I ever saw, rivaling that of a professional. The audience was very brilliant, the President of the Confederacy, Mr. Davis, Judah P. Benjamin, and others of equal distinction being present.

.   .   .   .   .   .

Mr. Davis, at the Executive Mansion, held weekly receptions, to which the public was admitted. These continued until nearly the end of the war. The occasions were not especially marked, but Mr. and Mrs. Davis were always delightful hosts. **page 383/**

.   .   .   .   .   .

But in April, 1865, the Confederacy ceased to exist; it passed into history, and Richmond was occupied by the Northern army. Many of its people were without food and without money — I mean money of the United States. It was at this period that the colored people of Richmond, slaves up to the time the war ended, but now no longer bondsmen, showed their loyalty and love for their former masters and mistresses. They, of course, had access to the commissary of the United States, and many, very many, of these former negro slaves, went to the United States Commissary, obtained food seemingly for themselves, and took it in basketfuls to their former owners, who were without food or money.   **page 386/**

No. 176   John S. Wise, *The End of an Era,* Boston, Houghton Mifflin Company, 1902.

It is a merciful provision of Providence which supplies diversion to mankind in the most desperate of situations. In the beleaguered capital, even amid the darkest hours of our fortunes, there were hearts throbbing with old emotions which banish thoughts of grief; and places where people met, clothed in the impenetrable armor of youth and joy, to dance and laugh adversity to scorn. War, pestilence, and famine are impotent to slay, infect, or starve the little naked archer.

Richmond was filled with young girls betrothed to young officers in the trenches about that city and Petersburg. It was not surprising, for never did a city of its population contain more beautiful and brilliant women than did Richmond of that time.   **page 396/**

The wedding bells chimed merrily in the wintry air for the coming nuptials of Colonel William B. Tabb, 59th Virginia Infantry, Wise's Brigade, and Miss Emily Rutherford.

.   .   .   .   .   .

The scene at the church was far more brilliant than one would fancy it could be after the descriptions given. Few girls with any social pretensions in Richmond had failed to wheedle or cajole some admiring blockade-running magnate into fetching them a silk or ribbon or feather from the outside world for this occasion. These blockade-runners were the only nabobs in the place: carrying their fortunes, their liberty, and sometimes their lives in their hands, they alone seemed possessors of the secret wherewith, even amidst poverty and want, to conjure up wealth and luxury. They still wore broadcloth and fine linen, drank French brandy, and smoked black   page 397/   cigars. To them, and them alone, could bride and bridesmaids, matrons and maid, look for the brave toggery so essential upon occasions like this; and the sea-dogs had not failed their fair dependents.

To me, the Tabb-Rutherford nuptials was an event of a lifetime; it had been years since I had seen such a gorgeous function. . . .   page 398/

It was not without grave misgivings that I stepped forth attired for the wedding. The length of Barksdale's [a person from whom he had borrowed a coat for the affair] waist was such that the bottom buttons of that coat somewhat constrained the movement of my hips; the coat-tails nearly reached my ankles; as for the sleeves, I was fortunate to get occasional glances at my finger-tips. The whole effect was to give me the appearance of a giant in body, a dwarf in legs, and an unfortunate who had lost both hands. . . .

But what cared I? I would have gone in a meal-sack. The larger the coat, the better; it gave more commodious opportunity to fill it with Mr. Rutherford's good cheer. At church, the judicious handling of a military cape veiled somewhat this extraordinary outfit; but when the house was reached no subterfuges longer availed. We   page 399/   stood revealed and undisguised, such as we were. If my appearance was extraordinary, in the vernacular of today, "there were others." The men had misfits of many makes; some even displayed patches. As for the costumes of the ladies, they were wonderful to behold. They seemed to have ransacked every old trunk in the garrets of Richmond, and some had actually utilized the lace and damask window-curtains of peacetimes. But a jollier and happier seeming throng was never assembled. . . . Who were there? Everybody that was anybody.

There was Mr. President Davis: he was assuredly a very clean-looking man; his manners were those of a dignified, gracious gentleman accustomed to good society. He claimed his tribute kiss from the bride, and well he might, for seldom had he culled one more sweet or pure. From the blushing girl he turned with a gracious compliment to her husband: "For a bride like that, colonel, you may demand a week's extension of your leave." Mr. Davis looked thin and careworn. Naturally refined in his appearance, his hair and beard were bleaching rapidly; and his bloodless cheeks and slender nose, with its clear-cut flat nostril, gave him almost the appearance of emaciation. Yet his eye was bright, his smile was winning, and manner most attractive. When   page 400/   he chose to be deferential and kindly, no man could excel him. When strongly moved, few men of his day surpassed him in eloquence. On occasion, he could touch the popular heart with a master hand. On his arm was Mrs. Davis, his very opposite in physique, looking as if, to use an old expression, "the gray mare was the better horse." Physically, she was large and looked well fed. Among us "Irreverents" it was believed that Mrs. Davis possessed great influence over her husband, even to the point that she could secure promotion for us, if she liked. She was intensely loyal to him, took no pains to conceal her pride in him, and was, perhaps, a trifle quick to show resentment towards those not as enthusiastic as she thought they should be in their estimate of his abilities. She had, among those who knew her best, warm, enthusiastic friends.

Close upon these came young Burton Harrison, the President's private secretary, looking like a fashion plate in his perfect outfit. Harrison was popular, and everybody had some cordial inquiry as to how he maintained such an immaculate wardrobe, when all the world besides was in rags. . . .

When Breckenridge, Secretary of War, strode up, he brought the perfume of Kentucky Bourbon with him. . . . There was a frankness of the soldier, the breadth of the statesman, the heartiness and courtesy to woman, of the Southern man of the world, in his every look and word.

The oleaginous Benjamin, Secretary of State, next glided in, his keg-like form and over-deferential manner   **page 401/**   suggestive of a prosperous shopkeeper. But his eye redeemed him, and his speech was elegantly polished, even if his nose was hooked and his thick lips shone red amidst the curly black of his Semitic beard. . . .

Then bluff old Secretary Mallory of the Navy came, — with no studied speech, but manly, frank, and kind, — one of the most popular members of the Confederate Congress. After him, Postmaster-General Regan [sic], of Texas, a large, plain-looking citizen, of more than ordinary common sense, but ill at ease in gatherings like this, and looking as if he might have left his carry-log and yoke of oxen at the door.

And so it went. . . .   **page 402/**

.   .   .   .   .   .

"And who are the ladies of the coterie?"

"Oh, . . . that is what we call the White House set. The two large girls in white are the Misses Howell, sisters of Mrs. Davis. The handsome blonde is the daughter of Senator Wigfall, of Texas; the striking girl in pink is Miss Campbell, daughter of the Confederate Chief Justice, Judge Campbell, of New Orleans."
page 403/

.   .   .   .   .   .

As I saw them, it seemed to me that the men entrusted with the civic administration of the Confederate government were not of as fine clay as her immortal soldiers, nor was it, I believe, a mere boyish fancy. Time has deepened the impression. . . .
page 404/

.   .   .   .   .   .

About midnight, a new and distinct coterie of guests arrived.

They were a party of *bon-vivant* friends of the host. By one means or another, this band secured the best to be had. To this feast of their companion, each and all had made their contribution. And now they had come to join him in celebrating the happy event of his daughter's marriage, and to partake of his good cheer.

There was big John Carvell, the Canadian blockade-runner, who had sent a few bottles of champagne, — a luxury then almost beyond price; and Major Robert Ould, the Confederate Commissioner of Exchange of Prisoners, who never failed to secure for himself on his trip down the river to meet the Union Commissioners of Exchange, an ample supply of the best food and drink; and Major "Buck" Allen of Claremont, whose cellars were still unexhausted. . . .

There was an air of business about these men. They   **page 409/**   had come for good cheer. What of creature comforts they did not secure was simply not to be had. What this party enjoyed in their private room, what cigars they smoked, what games they played with their host, how long they stayed, is beyond my ken. All that we lesser lights knew was that they had the reputation of being the only habitually well-fed and luxurious citizens of Richmond.

Supper for the general public was announced in due time, and, doubt it as you may, it was a sumptuous repast.

There were no sweets and ices, such as are seen in piping times of peace. But there was ornamentation! The pyramids, built of little balls of butter, were really pretty. They towered like the spun sugar, and nougat, or divided oranges, we see today. And great piles of rosy apples gave color to the feast. Terrapin, canvas-back ducks, patés, and the like were missing. Our friends, the enemy, had even cut us off from oysters. But there were turkeys and hams and delicious breads, and most beautifully stuffed eggs, and great piles of smoking sausages, and dishes of unsurpassed domestic pickles. There were no oils for salads, no sugar for preserves. Some one had given the bride a wedding present of coffee, and the rooms were filled with its delightful aroma. This we drank sugarless with great gusto. Great bowls of apple toddy, hot and cold, filled with roasted pippins, stood on the tables, and furnished all needful warmth and cheerfulness for any wedding feast.

So you see, dear readers, that, even to the last, there were times and places in the Confederacy where we got together and did like other and more prosperous folk, —

"Eat, drink, and be merry, for tomorrow you die." **page 410/**

No. 177 Judith W. McGuire, *Diary of a Southern Refugee,* New York, E. J. Hale & Son, 1867.

December 26, 1864: We extended ourselves [to be cheerful on Christmas Day]. The Church Services in the morning were sweet and comforting. St. Paul's was dressed most elaborately and beautifully with evergreens; all looked as usual; but there is much sadness on account of the failure of the South to keep Sherman back. When we got home our family circle was small, but pleasant. The Christmas turkey and ham were not. We had aspired to a turkey, but finding the prices range from $50 to $100 in the market on Saturday, we contented ourselves with roast-beef and the various   **page 323/**   little dishes which Confederate times have made us believe are tolerable substitutes for the viands of better days. At night I treated our little party to tea and ginger cakes — two very rare indulgences; and but for the sorghum, grown in our own fields, the cakes would be an impossible indulgence. Nothing but the well-ascertained fact that Christmas comes but once a year would make such extravagance at all excusable. We propose to have a family gathering when the girls come home, on the day before or after New Year's day (as that day will come on Sunday), to enjoy together, and with one or two refugee friends, the contents of a box sent the girls by a young officer who captured it from the enemy, consisting of white sugar, raisins, preserves, pickles, spices, etc. They threaten to give us a plum-cake, and I hope they will carry it out, particularly if we have any of our army friends with us. Poor fellows, how they enjoy our plain dinners when they come, and how we love to see them enjoy them! Two meals a day has become the universal system among the refugees, and many citizens, from necessity. The want of our accustomed tea or coffee is very much felt by the elders. The rule with us is only to have tea when sickness makes it necessary, and the headaches gotten up about dark have become the joke of the family. A country lady from one of the few spots in all Virginia where the enemy has never been, and consequently where they retain their comforts, asked me gravely why we did not substitute milk for tea. She could scarcely believe me when I told her that we had not had milk more than twice in eighteen months, and then it was sent by a country friend. It is now $4 a quart. page 324/

No. 178 Virginia Tunstall Clay, *A Belle of the Fifties*, New York, Doubleday, Page and Company, 1905.

> *[Early in the spring of 1864 Mr. Clay accepted a diplomatic mission to Canada. Mrs. Clay stayed with various friends and did not accompany him.]*

. . . I despatched a note of inquiry to Richmond, begging Mr. Davis to write to Mr. Seward to secure my safe passage by land to Canada. I told him of my unrest . . . and my desire to join my husband. The President's reply was reassuring and full of the confidence which sustained him to the end of the remaining days of the Confederacy. "There is no danger in coming here now," ran his message from the capital, dated December 29, 1864. "When Mr. Clay returns he will, of course, visit this place, and can conveniently meet you here." But when I proposed to try to make my way to this haven, Colonel Clay [one of her husband's brothers] wrote excitedly, animated by an anxiety as great as my own: page 238/ "Don't come to Richmond! Don't send the President letters or telegrams. He is in a sea of trouble, and has no time or thought for anything except the safety of the country. I fear the Congress is turning madly against him. It is the old story of the sick lion whom even the jackass can kick without fear. It is a very struggle for life with him. I do not know that he has any reliable friends in Congress, who will sustain him upon principle, fearlessly and ably. He has less and less power to intimidate his enemies, and they grow more numerous every day. . . . If he were preeminently gifted in all respects, the present moment is perilous enough to call forth all his energies no matter how great. . . . page 239/

No. 179 Sallie A. Brock Putnam, *Richmond During the War*, New York, G. W. Carleton and Company, 1867.

Richmond was growing rusty, dilapidated, and began to assume a war-worn appearance. Very few of the buildings had been brightened by a fresh application of paint since the commencement of hostilities, and where a plank fell off or a screw got loose, or a gate fell from its hinges, or a bolt gave way, or a lock was broken, it was most likely to remain for a time unrepaired; for the majority of our mechanics were in the field, and those left in the city were generally in the employ of the government, and we were forced to wait for a needful job, until patience would become almost exhausted. **page 315/**

1865

---

*"My native land, good-night!"**

Died: Confederacy, Southern. — At the late residence of his father, J. Davis, Richmond, Virginia, Southern Confederacy, aged 4 years. Death caused by strangulation. No funeral.†

---

*Judith W. McGuire, *Diary of a Southern Refugee*, New York, E. J. Hale & Son, 1867, p. 360.

†*Evening Whig*, Richmond, Virginia, April 7, 1865, p. 1.

No. 180 Sallie A. Brock Putnam, *Richmond During the War*, New York, G. W. Carleton and Company, 1867.

The New Year [1865] was ushered in with no better prospects. If there was no foreboding of the coming wreck of our coveted independence, we could at best only look forward to an indefinite continuation of the dire evils which had shrouded our land in sorrow and misery. Day by day our wants and privation increased. The supply of provisions in the city of Richmond was altogether inadequate to the demand, and generally of a quality that would have been altogether unappetizing in seasons of plenty. Every fresh encroachment of the enemy increased this scarcity, and in a proportionate ratio, the prices at which articles of food were held. There was also a great want of fuel. Those formerly accustomed to well heated houses, where comfort and luxury presided, now parsimoniously economized with a single ton of coal, or a single cord of wood to insure its lasting as long as possible, lest, when the last lump, or the last stick was consumed, no more could be obtained at any price. . . .

. . . It finally became an almost universal fashion in Richmond to permit "every day to take care of itself." **page 341/**

No. 181 George Cary Eggleston, *A Rebel's Recollections*, New York, G. P. Putnam's Sons, 1905.

In the cities, living was not by any means so easy as in the country. Business was paralyzed, and abundant as money was, it seems almost incredible that city people got enough of it to live on. Very many of them were employed, however, in various capacities, in the arsenals, departments, bureaus, etc., and these were allowed to buy rations at fixed rates, after the post-office clerks in Richmond had brought matters to a crisis by resigning their clerkships to go into the army, because they could not support life on their salaries of nine thousand dollars a year. For the rest, if people had anything to sell, they got enormous prices for it, and could live a while on the proceeds. Above all, a kindly, helpful spirit **page 95/** was developed by the common suffering and this, without doubt, kept many thousands of people from starvation. Those who had anything shared it freely with those who had nothing. There was no selfish looking forward, and no hoarding for the time to come. During those terrible last years, the future had nothing of pleasantness in its face, and people learned not to think of it at all. To get through today was the only care. Nobody formed any plans or laid by any money for tomorrow or next week or next year, and indeed to most of us there really seemed to be no future. I remember the start it gave me when a clergyman, visiting camp, asked a number of us whether our long stay in defensive works did not afford us an excellent opportunity to study with a view to our professional life after the war. We were not used to think of ourselves as possible survivors of a struggle which was every day perceptibly thinning our ranks. **page 96/** The coming of ultimate failure we saw clearly enough, but the future beyond was a blank. The subject was naturally not a pleasant one, and by common consent it was always avoided in conversation, until at last we learned to avoid it in thought as well. We waited gloomily for the end, but did not care to speculate upon the question when and how the end was to come. There was a vague longing for rest, which found now and then vent in wild newspaper stories of signs and omens portending the close of the war, but beyond this the matter was hardly ever discussed. We had early forbidden ourselves to think of any end to the struggle except a successful one, and that being now an impossibility, we avoided the subject altogether. **page 97/**

No. 182   Mary Boykin Chesnut, *A Diary from Dixie,* Boston, Houghton Mifflin Company, 1949.

January 17, 1865: Here is startling news. Politely but firmly, the Virginia legislature requests Jeff Davis and all of his cabinet to resign. Breckenridge is to take Seddon's portfolio. He will be War Minister. If we had had Breckenridge in Walker's place in the beginning, what a difference it might have made: Walker, who ruined us almost before we were under way. Clay of Alabama is responsible for that Walker, for Manassas and all that stupidity in not following up the victory. **page 473/**

No. 183   Constance Cary Harrison, *Recollections, Grave and Gay,* New York, Charles Scribner's Sons, 1912.

The engagement of my cousin Hetty Cary to Brigadier-General John Pegram having been announced, their decision to be married on January 19 was a subject of active interest. . . . On the evening of January 19 all our little world flocked to St. Paul's Church to see the nuptials of one called by many the most beautiful woman of the South, with a son of Richmond universally honored and beloved. Two days before, I being confined to my room with a cold, Hetty had come, bringing her bridal veil that I, with our mothers, might be the first to see it tried on her lovely crown of auburn hair. As she turned from the mirror to salute us with a charming blush and smile, the mirror fell and was broken to small fragments, an accident afterwards spoken of by the superstitious as one of a strange series of ominous happenings.

While a congregation that crowded floor and galleries of the church waited an

unusually long time for the arrival of bride and groom, my aunt and the other
page 201/ members of our family being already in our seats, I stood in the
vestibule outside with Burton Harrison and Colonel L. Q. C. Lamar, speculating
rather uneasily upon the cause of the delay. Mr. Harrison told us that Mrs. Davis
(who tenderly loved and admired the bride) had begged to be allowed to send the
President's carriage to drive her to the church, and he was sure that it had been in
prompt attendance at the bride's residence. Directly after, a shabby old Richmond
hack drove up, halting before the church, and from it issued the bride and groom,
looking a little perturbed, explaining that at the moment of setting out the President's
horses had reared violently, refusing to go forward, and could not be controlled, so
that they had been forced to get out of the carriage and send for another vehicle, at
that date almost impossible to secure in Richmond.

When the noble-looking young couple crossed the threshold of the church, my
cousin dropped her lace handkerchief and, nobody perceiving it, stooped forward to
pick it up, tearing the tulle veil over her face to almost its full length, then, regaining
herself, walked with a slow and stately step toward the altar. . . . After the ceremony we, her nearest, crowded around the couple, wishing them the best happi-
ness our loving hearts could picture. General Pegram's mother, brothers, page 202/
and sisters did the same; then, as they passed out, all eyes followed them with real
kindness and unalloyed good feeling. There was but a small reception afterward,
but one felt in the atmosphere a sense of sincere gladness in happy love, very rare
on such occasions.

Three weeks later, to the day, General Pegram's coffin, crossed with a victor's
palms beside his soldier's accoutrements, occupied the spot in the chancel where he
had stood to be married. Beside it knelt his widow swathed in crepe. Again Dr.
Minnegerode [sic] conducted the ceremony, again the church was full. Behind the
hearse, waiting outside, stood his war charger, with boots in stirrups. The wailing
of the band that went with us on the slow pilgrimage to Hollywood will never die
out of my memory. Burton Harrison drove in the carriage with me and my mother,
my poor cousin with her mother, brother, and General Custis Lee, her husband's
intimate friend, who stood beside her, as, leaning on her brother's arm, she remained
during the service close to the grave. General Pegram's family clustered beyond her.
Snow lay white on the hill-sides, the bare trees stretched their arms above us, the
river kept up its ceaseless rush and tumble, so much a part of daily life in our four
years of ordeal that we had grown accustomed to interpret its voice according to our
joy or grief. page 203/

No. 184 James D. Richardson, editor, *Messages and Papers of the Confederacy*,
Nashville, United States Printing Company, 1905, vol. I (2 vols.), p. 517.

Executive Office, Richmond, Va., January 24, 1865.
Gentlemen of the "Joint Committee on the State of the Country."
I have the honor to acknowledge receipt of resolutions adopted by the General

Assembly of Virginia in relation to certain restrictions said to have been placed on the transportation of supplies of food to the cities of Richmond and Petersburg.

Upon investigation I find that no orders have emanated from the War Department or the Provost Marshal of Richmond of the character supposed in the resolution. I, however, learn that there may be an order of the character spoken of emanating from the lieutenant general commanding the Confederate forces on the north side of the James River, which, if so, will be ascertained at once, he having been furnished with a copy of the resolution and called upon for information touching the same.

I am, gentlemen, very respectfully, your most obedient servant,

Jefferson Davis

No. 185 Daily Dispatch, Richmond, Virginia, February 3, 1865, p. 1.

General Lee Commander in Chief

The appointment of General Lee to the Command-in-Chief of the Armies of the Confederacy will give universal satisfaction, and inspire fresh confidence in every bosom. The President has shown, in this important act, a just appreciation of the exigencies of the situation, and a patriotic sympathy with the public sentiment, which pointed with entire unanimity to such a step.

We need say nothing of the great qualities which recommend General Lee to his present position. They have been tested in the fiery furnace, seven times heated, of a war which in its ferocity, duration and magnitude, has few parallels in history. . . . We do no wrong to the memory of Washington, nor to the facts of history, when we say that he never gave such proof of military ability as General Lee — a soldier who, with limited means, has successfully resisted for four years the enormous power of the United States, and kept the Confederate flag flying defiant on the Capitol.

. . . we have seen so much of popular impatience and fickleness, we appreciate so strongly the difficulties of General Lee's position, that we feel constrained to invoke the people to economize their enthusiasm, and invest their surplus of that article in forebearance and charity, qualities which may be needed before this war is over. General Lee, great man that he is, is neither infallible, omniscient nor omnipotent. . . . Let us not waste our breath at the beginning of General Lee's new career, but retain a portion of it to sustain him at the pinch of the hill. Let us show our admiration and confidence by holding up his hands, by strengthening his armies, by refraining from the croaking that would paralyze his soldiers, by putting down the spirit of extortion and greed, and pouring out cheerful contributions of material aid to the cause. — The Government has given us General Lee as Commander-in-Chief — now let the people do their part and give General Lee the public spirit and unselfish patriotism of 1861. Then with the blessing of Heaven, we may look forward as confidently to the achievement of Confederate Independence as the rising of to-morrow's sun.

No. 186 Mrs. D. Giraud Wright, *A Southern Girl in '61,* New York, Doubleday, Page & Company, 1905.

No instance of the absolute faith of our people, even at this late day, in the success of our Cause, is more convincing than their investment of money in Confederate Bonds, during these last months of the war.

Many circumstances could be related in evidence of this fact; but one will suffice. My grandmother, in Providence, Rhode Island, had succeeded by some means in sending to us through the lines $1,000 in gold. Without a moment's hesitation this precious metal was transmitted into Confederate bank notes, a large package of which, consisting of 500- and 100-dollar bills I have with me now, a constant reminder of the implicit faith in the success of the good Cause that was lost. I am sure my father would have felt he was recreant to his country if he had admitted to himself that Confederate money was not as good **page 221/** as gold. It may not have been the wisdom of this world, but it was beautiful, and I am glad he did it and I keep my bank notes and shall leave them to those that come after me, as an infallible proof that the civilization of the Old South produced a race of men, who maintained what they believed to be their constitutional rights, sacrificed every material gain, and, giving freely of their own lives and the lives of their sons, would not withhold the baser treasures of silver and gold. **page 222/**

No. 187 Mrs. D. Giraud Wright, *A Southern Girl in '61,* New York, Doubleday, Page & Company, 1905.

It seems almost incredible and yet it is a fact that several entertainments were given in Richmond in January and February, 1865. The most notable of these was at the beautiful home of the Welfords which was filled with guests who danced at what, I believe, was the last ball of the Confederacy. Grandmothers' satins and brocades figured on the occasion; and I warrant no lovelier group of women, nor company of more gallant gentlemen, were ever gathered. How the fiddlers scraped and the music swelled for "the dancers dancing in tune;" while they shut their ears and would not hear the minor key that wailed the ruin of our hopes. And the grim shade of Appomattox, looming dark already on the horizon, stalked ever nearer and nearer. **page 241/**

No. 188 John B. Jones, *A Rebel War Clerk's Diary*, New York, Old Hickory Bookshop, 1935, vol. II (2 vols.).

February 5, 1865: This fruitless mission [Peace Commission] will be fraught with evil, unless the career of Sherman be checked; and in that event the BATTLE for RICHMOND, and Virginia, and the Confederacy, will occur within a few months — perhaps weeks. The sooner the better for us, as delay will only serve to organize the Union Party sure to spring up; for many of the people are not only weary of the war, but they have no longer any faith in the President, his cabinet, Congress, the commissaries, quartermasters, enrolling officers, and most of the generals. **page 410/**

No. 189 *Daily Dispatch*, Richmond, Virginia, March 2, 1865, p. 4.

The Markets

Owing to certain groundless reports which have gained circulation in Richmond for the past few days, a large number of country people have been deterred from bringing their products to market, and, as a consequence, but little is offered at those places for sale. That further injury may not ensue from these rumors, we hereby contradict them upon the very highest official authority.

No. 190 *Daily Dispatch*, Richmond, Virginia, March 16, 1865, p. 1.

The *Dispatch* is published this morning on half a sheet only, because of the fact that all our employees — printers, reporters, and clerks — are members of military organizations, and were called out, yesterday by the Governor, to perform special services for a short time. . . .

No. 191 *Daily Dispatch*, Richmond, Virginia, March 18, 1865, p. 1.

Confederate States of America
War Department

Adjutant and Inspector General's Office,
Richmond, Virginia, March 15, 1865
Sirs, — You are hereby authorized to raise a Company or Companies of Negro Soldiers, under the provisions of the act of Congress, approved March 13, 1865.

When the requisite number shall have been recruited, they will be mustered into the service for the war, and muster rolls forwarded to this office.

The Companies, when organized, will be subject to the rules and regulations governing the Provisional Army of the Confederate States.

By command of the Secretary of War.

Signed,
John W. Reily, A.A.G.

To Maj. J. W. Pegram, and Maj. Thomas P. Turner, through Gen. Ewell.

No. 192 *Southern Historical Society Papers*, Richmond, Virginia, 1876-1943, vol. XIX (49 vols.).

[From the New York *Herald*, March 13, 1891.]

I [unidentified narrator] chanced to be in Richmond just three weeks previous to the surrender. Business had made me a frequent visitor to the metropolis of the Confederacy during the war, and I could tell quite accurately always how the war was going by the countenance and demeanor of its inhabitants, which to me were a more certain criterion than the daily papers. . . .

As soon, therefore, as I stepped from the train on the occasion referred to, I knew that something was wrong; there seemed a death-like stillness to pervade the city; everyone wore a haggard, scared look, as if in apprehension of some great impending calamity. I dared not ask a question, nor had I need to do so, as I felt too surely that the end was near. My first visit was to my banker, one who dealt largely in Confederate securities, and knew too well the ups and downs of the Confederate cause by the fluctuations of its paper. As soon as he could give me a private moment he said in a sad, low tone:

"If you have any paper money put it into specie at once."   page 329/

"Is it as bad as that?" I replied.

"Yes, and much worse; another week and you will get nothing."

As I happened to have about three thousand dollars in Confederate paper, I drew it forth and requested him to get me what silver it would bring.

The next morning he handed me thirty dollars, telling me at the same time to feel thankful for that much.

At a house of a friend with whom I was staying I asked the question, "How do you think this war will terminate?" The host simply took me to his bedroom, and raising the coverlet, showed me several barrels of flour, sacks of coffee, sugar, and other groceries snugly stowed away. This, he said, I would find to be the case in nearly every household in the city. In every store I entered there seemed to be the greatest scarcity of goods, and a disinclination to sell. . . .   **page 330/**

No. 193   John B. Jones, *A Rebel War Clerk's Diary,* New York, Old Hickory Bookshop, 1935, vol. II (2 vols.).

March 24, 1865: Clear and very windy. The fear of utter famine is now assuming form. Those who have the means are laying up stores for the day of siege, — I mean a closer and more rigorous **page 457/**   siege, — when all communications with the country shall cease; and this makes the commodities scarcer and the prices higher. There is a project on foot to send away some thousands of useless consumers; but how it is to be affected [sic] by the city authorities, and where they will be sent to, are questions I have not heard answered. The population of the city is not less than 100,000, and the markets cannot subsist 70,000. Then there is the army in the vicinity, which *must* be fed. I suppose the poultry and the sheep will be eaten, and something like a pro rata distribution of flour and meal ordered.

There is a rumor of a great victory by Gen. Johnston in North Carolina, the taking of 4500 prisoners, 70 guns, etc., — merely a rumor, I am sure. On the contrary, I apprehend that we shall soon have news of the capture of Raleigh by Sherman. Should this be our fate, we shall soon have three or four different armies encompassing us!

I tried in vain this morning to buy a small fish-hook; but could not find one in the city. None but coarse large ones are in the stores. A friend has promised me one — and I can make *pin-hooks,* that will catch minnows. I am too skillful an angler to starve where water runs; and even minnows can be eaten. Besides, there are eels and catfish in the river. The water is always muddy. **page 458/**

No. 194   John B. Jones, *A Rebel War Clerk's Diary,* New York, Old Hickory Bookshop, 1935, vol. II (2 vols.).

April 1, 1865: I have leave of absence, to improve my health; and propose accompanying my daughter Anne, next week, to Mr. Hobson's mansion in Goochland County. The Hobsons are opulent, and she will have an excellent asylum there, if the vicissitudes of the war do not spoil her calculations. I shall look for angling streams; and if successful, hope for both sport and better health. **page 464/**

No. 195 Robert Underwood Johnson and Clarence Clough Buel (eds.), *Battles and Leaders of the Civil War,* New York, The Century Company, 1887, vol. IV (4 vols.).

The Fall of Richmond

I. The Evacuation. — By Clement Sulivane, Captain, C.S.A.

About 11:30 A.M. on Sunday, April 2d, a strange agitation was perceptible on the streets of Richmond, and within half an hour it was known on all sides that Lee's lines had been broken below Petersburg; that he was in full retreat on Danville; that the troops covering the city at Chaffin's and Drewry's Bluffs were on the point of being withdrawn, and that the city was forthwith to be abandoned. A singular security had been felt by the citizens of Richmond, so the news fell like a bomb-shell in a peaceful camp, and dismay reigned supreme.

All that Sabbath day the trains came and went, wagons, vehicles, and horsemen rumbled and dashed to and fro, and, in the evening ominous groups of ruffians — more or less in liquor — began to make their appearance on the principal thorough-fares of the city. As night came on pillaging and rioting and robbing took place. The police and a few soldiers were on hand, and, after the arrest of a few ringlead-ers and the more riotous of their followers, a fair degree of order was restored. But Richmond saw few sleeping eyes during the pandemonium of that night.

The division of Major-General G. W. C. Lee, of Ewell's corps, at that time rested in the trenches eight miles below Richmond, with its right on the James River, cover-ing Chaffin's Bluff. I was at the time its assistant adjutant-general, and was in the city on some detached duty connected with the "Local Brigade" belonging to the division, — a force composed of soldiers of the army, detailed on account of their mechanical skill to work in the arsenals, etc., and of clerks and other employees of the War, Treasury, Quartermaster, and other departments.

Upon receipt of the news from Petersburg I reported to General Ewell (then in Richmond) for instructions, and was ordered to assemble and command the Local Brigade, cause it to be well supplied with ammunition and provisions, and await further orders. All that day and night I was engaged in this duty, but with small result, as the battalions melted away as fast as they were formed, mainly under orders from the heads of the departments who needed all their employees in the transportation and guarding of the archives, etc., but partly, no doubt, from desertions. When morning dawned fewer than 200 men remained under command of Captain Edward Mayo.

Shortly before day General Ewell rode in person to my headquarters and in-formed me that General G. W. C. Lee was then crossing the pontoon at Drewry's; that he would destroy it and press on to join the main army; that all the bridges over the river had been destroyed, except Mayo's, between Richmond and Manchester, and that the wagon bridge over the canal in front of Mayo's had already been burned by Union emissaries. My command was to hasten to Mayo's bridge and protect it, and the one remaining foot-bridge over the canal leading to it, until General Gary, of South Carolina, should arrive. I hurried to my command, and fifteen minutes later occupied Mayo's bridge at the foot of 14th street, and made military dispositions to protect it to the last extremity. This done, I had nothing to do but listen for sounds and gaze on the terrible splendor of the scene. And such a scene probably the world has seldom witnessed. Either incendiaries, or (more probably) fragments of bombs from the arsenals, had fired various buildings, and the two cities, Richmond and Manchester, were like a blaze of day amid the surrounding darkness. Three high-arched bridges were in flames; beneath them the waters sparkled and dashed and rushed on by the burning city. Every now and then as a magazine exploded, a column of white smoke rose up as high as the eye could reach, instantaneously followed by a deafening sound. The earth seemed to rock and tremble as with the shock of an earthquake, and immediately afterwards hundreds of shells would explode in air and send their iron spray down far below the bridge. As the immense magazines of   **page 725/**   cartridges ignited the rattle as of thousands of musketry would follow, and then all was still for the moment, except the dull roar and crackle of the fast-spreading fires. At dawn we heard terrific explosions about "The Rocketts" from the unfinished iron-clads down the river.

By daylight, on the 3d, a mob of men, women, and children, to the number of several thousands, had gathered at the corner of 14th and Cary streets and other outlets, in front of the bridge, attracted by the vast commissary depot at that point; for it must be remembered that in 1865 Richmond was a half-starved city, and the Confederate Government had that morning removed its guards and abandoned the removal of the provisions, which was impossible for the want of transportation. The depot doors were forced open and a demoniacal struggle for the countless barrels of hams, bacon, whiskey, flour, sugar, coffee, etc., etc., raged about the building among the hungry mob. The gutters ran whiskey, and it was lapped as it flowed down the streets, while all fought for a share of the plunder. The flames came nearer and nearer, and at last caught in the commissariat itself.

At daylight the approach of the Union forces could be plainly discerned. After a little came the clatter of horses' hoofs galloping up Main street. My infantry guard stood to arms, the picket across the canal was withdrawn, and the engineer officer lighted a torch of fat pine. By direction of the Engineer Department barrels of tar, surrounded by pine-knots, had been placed at intervals on the bridge, with kerosene at hand, and a lieutenant of engineers had reported for the duty of firing them at my order. The noisy train proved to be Gary's ambulances, sent forward preparatory to his final rush for the bridge. The muleteers galloped their animals about half-way down, when they were stopped by the dense mass of human beings. Rapidly communicating to Captain Mayo my instructions from General Ewell, I ordered that officer to stand firm at his post until Gary got up. I rode forward into the mob and cleared a lane. The ambulances were galloped down to the bridge, I retired to my post, and the mob closed in after me and resumed its wild struggle for plunder. A few minutes later a long line of cavalry in gray turned into 14th street, and sword in hand galloped straight down to the river; Gary had come. The mob scattered right and left before the armed horsemen, who reined up at the canal.

Presently a single company of cavalry appeared in sight, and rode at head-long speed to the bridge. "My rear-guard," explained Gary. Touching his hat to me he called out, "All over, goodbye; blow her to h—ll," and trotted over the bridge. That was the first and last I ever saw of General Gary, of South Carolina.

In less than sixty seconds Captain Mayo was in column of march, and as he reached the little island about half way across the bridge, the single piece of artillery, loaded with grape-shot, that had occupied that spot, arrived on the Manchester side of the river. The engineer officer, Dr. Lyons, and I walked leisurely to the island, setting fire to the provided combustible matter as we passed along, and leaving the north section of Mayo's bridge wrapped in flames and smoke. At the island we stopped to take a view of the situation north of the river, and saw a line of blue-coated horsemen galloping in furious haste up Main street. Across 14th street they stopped, and then dashed down 14th street to the flaming bridge. They fired a few random shots at us three on the island, and we retreated to Manchester. I ordered my command forward, the lieutenant of engineers saluted and went about his business, and myself and my companion sat on our horses for nearly a half-hour, watching the occupation of Richmond. We saw another string of horsemen in blue pass up Main street, then we saw a dense column of infantry march by, seemingly without end; we heard the very welkin ring with cheers as the United States forces reached Capitol Square, and then we turned and slowly rode on our way. page 726/

No. 196 Edward A. Pollard, *The Lost Cause,* New York, E. B. Treat & Company, 1867.

It is a most remarkable circumstance that the people of Richmond had remained in profound ignorance of the fighting which had been taking place for three days on General Lee's lines. There was not a rumor of it in the air. Not a newspaper office in the city had any inkling of what was going on. Indeed for the past few days there had been visible reassurance in the Confederate Capital; there were rumors that Johnston was moving to Lee's lines and a general idea that the combined force would take the offensive against the enemy. . . .

. . . .

. . . the report of the evacuation of Richmond fell upon many incredulous ears. One could see the quiet streets stretching away, unmolested by one single gun of war; across the James the landscape glistened in the sun; everything which met the eye spoke of peace, and made it impossible to picture in the imagination the scene which was to ensue. There were but few people in the streets; no vehicles disturbed the quiet of the Sabbath; the sound of the church-going bells rose in the cloudless sky, and floated on the blue tide of the cloudless day. How was it possible to imagine that in the next twenty-four hours, war, with its train of horrors, was to enter the scene; that this peaceful city, a serene possession for four years, was at last to succumb; that it was to be a prey to a great conflagration, and that all the hopes of the Southern Confederacy were to be consumed in one day, as a scroll in the fire! page 693/

No. 197   John B. Jones, *A Rebel War Clerk's Diary*, New York, Old Hickory Bookshop, 1935, vol. II (2 vols.).

April 2, 1865: I hear nothing . . . at the department; but the absence of dispatches there is now interpreted as bad news! Certain it is, the marching of veteran troops from the defenses of Richmond, and replacing them hurriedly with militia, can only indicate an emergency of alarming importance. A decisive struggle is probably at hand — and may possibly be in progress while I write. Or there may be nothing in it — more than a precautionary concentration to preserve our communications.

    Mrs. Davis sold nearly all her movables — including presents — before leaving the city. She sent them to different stores. . . . The excited women in this neighborhood say they have learned the city is to be evacuated tonight.

    It is true! The enemy have broken through our lines and attained the South Side Road. Gen. Lee has dispatched the Secretary to have everything in readiness to *evacuate the city to-night.* The President told a lady that Lieut.-Gen. Hardee was only twelve miles distant and might get up in time to save the day. But then Sherman must be in *his* rear. There is no wild excitement — yet.   **page 465/**

     ·   ·   ·   ·   ·   ·

    At night. All is quiet. No explosion, no conflagration, no riots, etc. How long will this continue? When will the enemy come?

     ·   ·   ·   ·   ·   ·

    I remain here, broken in health and bankrupt in fortune, awaiting my fate, whatever it may be. I can do no more. If I could, I would.   **page 467/**

No. 198   Sallie A. Brock Putnam, *Richmond During the War*, New York, G. W. Carleton and Company, 1867.

    There is one class of the citizens of Richmond of whom too much cannot be said in praise, to whom too much gratitude cannot be accorded. The ministers of the gospel of the different religious denominations in the city, will be held in lasting **page 46/**   remembrance. They sustained our fainting hearts by their prayers, and example, and through the trials ever accumulating in number and heaviness, during four years of war.

    Universally holding sentiments of approval, or acquiescent sympathy in the cause of the South, they carefully avoided proclaiming them from the pulpit. No flags floated from our spires; military and religious insignia were not blended; our churches, though simple in construction and material decoration, were sanctified by the presence of the Holy Spirit.   **page 47/**

No. 199 Jefferson Davis, *The Rise and Fall of the Confederate Government,* Richmond, Virginia, Garrett and Massie, Inc., n.d., vol. II (2 vols.).

On Sunday, April 2d, while I was in St. Paul's Church, General Lee's telegram, announcing his speedy withdrawal from Petersburg and the consequent necessity for evacuating Richmond, was handed to me. I rose quietly and left the church. The occurrence probably attracted attention, but the people of Richmond had been too long beleaguered, had known me to receive too often notice of threatened attacks, and the congregation of St. Paul's was too refined, to make a scene at anticipated danger. For all these reasons, the reader will be prepared for the announcement that the sensational stories which have been   **page 566/** published about the agitation caused by my leaving the church during service were the creation of fertile imaginations. I went to my office and assembled the heads of departments and bureaus, as far as they could be found on a day when all the offices were closed, and gave the needful instructions for our removal that night, simultaneously with General Lee's withdrawal from Petersburg. The event was not unforeseen, and some preparation had been made for it, though, as it came sooner than was expected, there was yet much to be done. My own papers were disposed as usual for convenient reference in the transaction of current affairs, and as soon as the principal officers had left me the executive papers were arranged for removal. This occupied me and my staff until late in the afternoon. By this time the report that Richmond was to be evacuated had spread through the town, and many who saw me walking toward my residence left their houses to inquire whether the report was true. Upon my admission of the painful fact — qualified, however, by the expression of my hope that we would return under better auspices — the ladies especially with generous sympathy and patriotic impulse, responded, "If the success of the cause requires you to give up Richmond, we are content."   **page 567/**

No. 200 Elizabeth Wright Weddell, *St. Paul's Church, Its Historic Years and Memorials,* Richmond, Virginia, The William Byrd Press, 1931, vol. 1 (2 vols.).

[From a description of Mr. Davis' receiving the evacuation message from General Lee on April 2, 1865, by Dr. Minnigerode.]

It was Sunday, like that of the First Manassas, and the air seemed full of something like a foreboding of good or bad. All expected a battle and I knew that wagons were held in readiness for transportation of commissary stores, ammunition, etc. The beautiful church of St. Paul, in its chaste simplicity and symmetry, was filled to the utmost, as always during the war. Mr. Davis who never failed to be in his pew unless when sick or absent from the city, was there, devoutly following the services of the church. It was the regular day for the Holy Communion. Nothing had occurred to disturb the congregation, though anxiety was in many a heart. As the Ante-communion service was read and the people were on their knees, I saw the sexton go to Mr. Davis's pew and hand him what proved to be a telegram. I could not but see it. Mr. Davis took it quietly, not to disturb the congregation, put on his overcoat, and walked out. On Communion occasions I was wont to make a short address from the chancel. While doing so, the sexton came in repeatedly and called out this one and that one, all connected with the government and military service. Of course the congregation became very restless, and I tried to finish my address as soon as I could, without adding to the threatening panic.

But when the sexton came to the chancel railing and page 243/ spoke to Reverend Mr. Kepler, who assisted me, they began to stir, and I closed as quickly as possible. Then Mr. Kepler told me that the provost-marshal wanted to see me in the vestry-room. I went out and found Major Isaac Carrington, who informed me that General Lee's lines had been broken before Petersburg, that he was in retreat, and Richmond must be evacuated. . . . I returned to the chancel. As I entered, I found the congregation streaming out of the church, and I sprang forward and called out, 'Stop! Stop! there is no necessity for leaving the church,' and most of them returned. . . . I requested the communicants to stay for the celebration. About two hundred and fifty or three hundred remained and some felt as if they were kneeling there with the halter around their necks. . . . page 244/

No. 201 *Southern Historical Society Papers,* Richmond, Virginia, 1876-1943, vol. XXIX (49 vols.).

> *[From the Richmond, Va., Dispatch, February 3, 1902. The following are excerpts from the reminiscences of an unidentified narrator of things which came under his personal observation.]*

As I recall that period, nothing seems more remarkable to me than the absolute surprise the fall of Richmond caused in Richmond itself. Whether or not it was anticipated by the government, I do not know; but there can be no doubt that outside of official circles — that is, to almost everyone in the city — the announcement came with an unexpectedness and surprise of an earthquake. page 152/

. . . .

There were no physical portents for superstition to feed on. On the contrary, the day was as perfect a day as Richmond had ever seen; the budding trees, the flowers of spring, the balmy atmosphere, the clear sky, bright sunlight, all combining to make it page 153/ a spring-day of unsurpassed loveliness, then, too, it was Sunday; and this, strange as it may seem, added somewhat to its quiet sweet brightness. Richmond had enough during those four years to make it sad, and there were, indeed, many mourners and much sorrow.

But in the midst of all this there was, as I recollect, much gayety also. This was not merely rejoicing over a victory which seemed to bring final success nearer, but that social gayety which nature demands, and in which, it would seem, a people must indulge, even when otherwise heavily oppressed. Thus it was that crowds promenaded on the Capitol Square, afternoon after afternoon, to music furnished by the government or the city, walking, talking, and laughing. In house after house the young people met at what were called "starvation parties" to enjoy "the feast of reason and the flow of soul," to dance and make merry, and to do, indeed, everything usual on such occasions except eat. Food was the severest problem in those days. Richmond laughed while it cried, and sang while it endured, and suffered and bled. With all the suffering in and around it, Richmond was yet not a sad place during the war. And of all days, taking it as a whole, there was none during which, in at least some respects, life assumed a more stirring and animated appearance than on Sunday. On this day the streets, especially in the resident portion of the city, were thronged with people, variously dressed, but all dressed in their best, going to some church, for Richmond was then, and still is, for aught I know, a great church going place. . . .   page 154/

. . . .

I do remember that before [that Sunday] closed there was a widespread impression that the rumors and fears of the early morning were false. When my father's friend, Dr. Harrison, came home that night, he told us it was a false alarm; that there had been a crisis, but it was   page 156/   safely passed. It may seem strange, but such was our unwillingness to believe the worst, and such our confidence in Lee and his army, that in the absence of any official announcement we all went to bed that night feeling little or no concern. I do not know how many others in the city did this, but we did, and, what is more, we slept the sleep of the just until suddenly awakened in the early hours of Monday morning by a tremendous shock, which rocked the house and rattled the windows. . . . Then we knew for sure that our fears of the day before were not idle fears.   page 157/

[The narrator went downtown to observe the fire and the pillaging, but when the arrival of Federal troops was announced, he started rapidly for home the most direct way, through Capitol Square.]

. . . and just as I reached the Washington Monument, I was little less than horrified to see the troops entering the Square through the main entrance facing Grace Street. In my youth I was not, at least notoriously either a bad or cowardly boy, but that sight, so new and unexpected, was rather too much for surprised nerves, and for one thing I quickly betook myself to the largest tree I could find and hid myself. Here I stood as the soldiers swept into the square, passed the Monument, and went on to the Capitol. It was then only a few minutes later — so my memory serves me — that I saw the United States flag appear on the flag-pole above, where the Stars and Bars had floated for years. Four years before this, on a day, I think, in this same month of April, my father, always a strong secessionist, had taken me to this same Square to a great meeting in ratification of the ordinance of secession, and I recollect to have seen the flag of the Confederacy raised on the Capitol where the Stars and Stripes had waved from time immemorial. Putting the two things together, I have often said that, as a boy, I saw the Alpha and the Omega — the beginning and the end — of the Southern Confederacy in Old Virginia. As to the first, I was, of course, too young to be in any way affected by it, but at the latter, I must say, as I stood behind that tree and saw what I saw, I remembered my dead soldier brother, what he had suffered for what he deemed right, and my young heart was filled with bitter hate, and my lips, which had never before uttered an oath, poured maledictions on our triumphant foes. Then I went home and so practically, closed those two days in my life, **page 159/** which of all others will ever stand forth as living, dreadful pictures before my mind. **page 160/**

No. 202   Edward M. Boykin, *The Falling Flag,* New York, E. J. Hale & Son, 1874.

Richmond had collected within its walls the refuse of the war — thieves and deserters, male and female, the vilest of the vile were there, but strict military discipline had kept it down. Now, in one moment, [the evacuation] it was all removed — all restraint was taken off — and you may imagine the consequences. There were said to be 5,000 deserters in the city, and you could see the gray jackets here and there sprinkled in the mob that was roaring down the street. When we reached somewhere between Twentieth and Twenty-fifth streets . . . the flames swept across Main street so that we could not cross. The column turned to the right and so we got into the street above it. On this (Franklin street) are many private residences; at the windows we could see the sad and tearful faces of the kind Virginia women, who had never failed the soldier in four long years of war and trouble, ready to the last to give him devoted attendance in his wounds and sickness, and to share with his necessities the last morsel. **page 13/**

No. 203   George Cary Eggleston, *A Rebel's Recollections,* New York, G. P. Putnam's Sons, 1905.

Many of [the women of the South] denied themselves not only delicacies, but substantial food also, when by enduring semi-starvation they could add to the stock of food at the command of the subsistence officers. I myself   **page 67/**   knew more than one household of women, who, from the moment that food began to grow scarce, refused to eat meat or drink coffee, living thenceforth only upon vegetables of a speedily perishable sort, in order that they might leave the more for the soldiers in the field. When a friend remonstrated with one of them, on the ground that her health, already frail, was breaking down utterly for want of proper diet, she replied in a quiet, determined way, "I know that very well; but it is little that I can do, and I must do that little at any cost. My health and my life are worth less than those of my brothers, and if they give theirs to the cause, why should not I do the same? I would starve to death cheerfully if I could feed one soldier more by doing so, but the things I eat can't be sent to camp. I think it a sin to eat anything that can be used for rations." And she meant what she said, too, as a little mound in the church-yard testifies. **page 68/**

No. 204 Robert Underwood Johnson and Clarence Clough Buel, (eds.), *Battles and Leaders of the Civil War*, New York, The Century Company, 1887, vol. IV (4 vols.).

The Fall of Richmond

II. The occupation. — By Thomas Thatcher Graves, Aide-de-camp on the staff of Gen. Weitzel.

In the spring of 1865 the total length of the lines of the Army of the James before Richmond (under General Godfrey Weitzel, commanding the Twenty-fifth Corps) was about eleven miles, not counting the cavalry front, and extending from the Appomattox River to the north side of the James. The Varina and New Market turnpikes passed directly through the lines into the city, which was the center of all our efforts.

About 2 o'clock on the morning of April 3d bright fires were seen in the direction of Richmond. Shortly after, while we were looking at these fires, we heard explosions, and soon a prisoner was sent in by General Kautz. The prisoner was a colored teamster, and he informed us that immediately after dark the enemy had begun making preparations to leave, and that they were sending all the teams to the rear. A forward movement of our entire picket line corroborated this report. As soon as it was light General Weitzel ordered Colonel E. E. Graves, senior aide-de-camp, and Major Atherton H. Stevens, Jr., provost-marshal, to take a detachment of forty men from the two companies (E and H) of the 4th Massachusetts Cavalry, and make a reconnaissance. Slowly this little band of scouts picked their way in. Soon after we moved up the New Market road at a slow pace.

As we approached the inner line of defenses we saw in the distance divisions of our troops, many of them upon the double-quick, aiming to be the first in the city; a white and colored division were having a regular race, the white troops on the turnpike and the colored in the fields. As we neared the city the fires seemed to increase in number and size, and at intervals loud explosions were heard.

On entering we found Capitol Square covered with people who had fled there to escape the fire and were utterly worn out with fatigue and fright.   page 726/ Details were at once made to scour the city and press into service every able-bodied man, either white or black, and make them assist in extinguishing the flames. General Devens's division marched into the city, stacked arms, and went to work. Parson's engineer company assisted by blowing up houses to check its advance, as about every engine was destroyed or rendered useless by the mob. In this manner the fire was extinguished and perfect order restored in an incredibly short time after we occupied the city. There was absolutely no plundering upon the part of our soldiers; orders were issued forbidding anything to be taken without remuneration, and no complaints were made of infringement of these orders. General G. F. Shepley was placed on duty as military governor. He had occupied a similar position in New Orleans after its capture in 1862, and was eminently fitted for it by education and experience. As we entered the suburbs the general ordered me to take half a dozen cavalry men and go to Libby Prison, for our thoughts were upon the wretched men whom we supposed were still confined within its walls. It was very early in the morning, and we were the first Union troops to arrive before Libby. Not a guard, not an inmate remained; the doors were wide open, and only a few negroes greeted us with, "Dey's all gone, massa!"

The next day after our entry into the city, on passing out from Clay street, from Jefferson Davis's house, I saw a crowd coming, headed by President Lincoln, who was walking with his usual long, careless stride, and looking about with an interested air and taking in everything. Upon my saluting he said: "Is it far to President Davis's house?" I accompanied him to the house, which was occupied by General Weitzel as headquarters. The President had arrived about 9 o'clock, at the landing called Rocketts, upon Admiral Porter's flagship, the *Malvern,* and as soon as the boat was made fast, without ceremony, he walked on shore and started off uptown. As soon as Admiral Porter was informed of it he ordered a guard of marines to follow as escort; but in the walk of about two miles they never saw him, and he was directed by negroes. At the Davis house, he was shown   **page 727/**   into the reception-room, with the remark that the housekeeper had said that the room was President Davis's office. As he seated himself he remarked, "This must have been President Davis's chair," and crossing his legs, he looked far off with a serious, dreamy expression. At length he asked me if the housekeeper was in the house. Upon learning that she had left, he jumped up and said with a boyish manner, "Come, let's look at the house!" We went pretty much over it; I retailed all that the housekeeper had told me, and he seemed interested in everything. As we came down the staircase General Weitzel came, in breathless haste, and at once President Lincoln's face lost its boyish expression as he realized that *duty* must be resumed. Soon afterwards Judge Campbell, and General Anderson (Confederates), and others called and asked for an interview with the President. It was granted, and took place in the parlor with closed doors.

I accompanied President Lincoln and General Weitzel to Libby Prison and Castle Thunder, and heard General Weitzel ask what he (General Weitzel) should do in regards to the conquered people. President Lincoln replied that he did not wish to give any orders on that subject, but, as he expressed it, "If I were in your place I'd let 'em up easy, let 'em up easy."

A few days after our entry General R. E. Lee surrendered, and early one morning we learned that he had just arrived at his house in the city. . . . **page 728/**

No. 205 *Official Records of the Union and Confederate Armies,* series I, volume XLVI, part III, Washington, Government Printing Office, 1894.

> Hdqrs. Dept. of Virginia, Army of the James,
> In the Field, April 3, 1865.*

General Weitzel, Commanding, Richmond:

You will seize what tobacco may be within reach to sell for the purpose of feeding the poor of the city. You are appointed governor of Richmond, and in my absence will act as commander of the department in all matters which require prompt action. Let food and necessaries come to the city; register the white men; appoint a military commission for the punishment of offenses against law and order; organize a police force. Start gas and water companies, and protect all inhabitants in their property who come forward and take the oath of allegiance on due notice. By property, persons are not meant. You will not allow any taxes to be imposed on rents paid other than necessary to recognize ownership of loyal landlords. Be your own treasury agent; allow men to open hotels, but not grog shops. **page 535/**

    *Another copy is dated April 4.

> E. O. C. Ord,
> Major-General, Commanding

No. 206 Judith W. McGuire, *Diary of a Southern Refugee,* New York, E. J. Dale & Son, 1867.

April 3, 1865: . . . We have **page 342/** passed through a fatal thirty-six hours. Yesterday morning (it seems a week ago) we went, as usual, to St. James's Church, hoping for a day of peace and quietness, as well as of religious improvement and enjoyment. How short-sighted we are and how little do we know of what is coming, either of judgment or mercy! . . . The services being over, we left the church and . . . not until then did I observe that every countenance was wild with excitement. The inquiry, "What is the matter?" ran from lip to lip. Nobody seemed to hear or to answer. An old friend ran across the street, pale with excitement, repeating . . . that unless we heard better news from General Lee the city would be evacuated. We could do nothing; no one suggested any thing to be done. We **page 343/** reached home with a strange, unrealizing feeling. . . . We began to understand that the government was moving and that the evacuation was indeed going on. The office-holders were now making arrangements to get off. Every car was ordered to be ready to take them South. . . . The people were rushing up and down the streets, vehicles of all kinds were flying along, bearing goods of all sorts and people of all ages and classes who could go beyond the corporation lines. . . . Last night when we went out to hire a servant to go to Camp Jackson for our sister, we for the first time realized that our money was worthless here, and that we are in fact penni-less. . . . The gentlemen walked down to the War Office in the night to see what was going on. Alas! every sight and sound was grievous and heavy.   **page 344/**

A telegram just received from General Lee hastened the evacuation. The public offices were all forsaken. They said that by three o'clock in the morning the work must be completed, and the city ready for the enemy to take possession. . . . About two o'clock in the morning we were startled by a loud sound like thunder; the house shook and the windows rattled; it seemed like an earthquake in our midst. We knew not what it was, nor did we care. It was soon understood to be the blowing up of a magazine below the city. In a few hours another exploded on the outskirts of the city, much louder than the first, and shivering innumerable plate-glass windows all over Shockoe Hill. It was then daylight, and we were standing out upon the pavement. . . . The lower part of the city was burning. About seven o'clock I set off to go to the central depot to see if the cars would go out. As I went from Franklin to Broad Street, and on Broad, the pavements were covered with broken glass; women both white and coloured, were walking in multitudes from the Commissary offices and burning stores with bags of flour, meal, coffee, sugar, rolls of cotton cloth, etc., coloured men were rolling wheel-barrows filled in the same way. . . . The rabble **page 345/** rushed by me in one stream. At last I exclaimed, "Who are those shouting? What is the matter?" I seemed to be answered by a hundred voices, "The Yankees have come." I turned to come home, but what was my horror, when I reached Ninth Street, to see a regiment of Yankee cavalry come dashing up, yelling, shouting, hallooing, screaming! All Bedlam let loose could not have vied with them in diabolical roarings. I stood riveted to the spot; I could not move nor speak. Then I saw the iron gates of our time-honoured and beautiful Capitol Square, on the walks and greensward of which no hoof had been allowed to tread, thrown open and cavalry dash in. I could see no more; I must go on with a mighty effort, or faint where I stood. . . . An hour or two after breakfast we all retired to our rooms exhausted. No one had slept; no one had sought repose or thought of their [sic] own comfort. The Federal soldiers were roaming about the streets; either whiskey or the excess of joy had given some of them the appearance of being beside themselves. We had hoped that very little whiskey would be found in the   **page 346/** city, as, by order of the Mayor, casks were emptied yesterday evening in the streets, and it flowed like water through the gutters; but the rabble had managed to find it secreted in the burning shops, and bore it away in pitchers and buckets. It soon became evident that protection would be necessary for the residences, and [since] ladies only were allowed to apply for guards, I must undertake it. . . .   **page 347/**

. . . [By three o'clock] the flames had decreased, but the business part of the city was in ruins. . . . Almost every house is guarded; and the streets are now (ten o'clock) perfectly quiet. The moon is shining brightly on our captivity. God guide and watch over us!   **page 349/**

No. 207 John B. Jones, *A Rebel War Clerk's Diary*, New York, Old Hickory Bookshop, 1935, vol. II (2 vols.).

April 3, 1865: Another clear and bright morning. It was a quiet night, with its millions of stars. And yet how few could sleep, in anticipation of the entrance of the enemy! But no enemy came until 9 A.M. when some 500 were posted at the Capitol Square. They had been waited upon previously by the City Council, and the surrender of the city stipulated — to occur this morning. They were asked to post guards for the protection of property from pillage, etc., and promised to do so.

At dawn there were two tremendous explosions, seeming to startle the earth, and crashing the glass throughout the western end of the city. One of these was the blowing up of the magazine, near the new almshouse — the other probably the destruction of an iron-clad ram. But subsequently there were others. I was sleeping soundly when awakened by them.   **page 467/**

.   .   .   .   .

At 8½ A.M. the armory, arsenal, and laboratory (Seventh and Canal Streets), which had been previously fired, gave forth terrific sounds from thousands of bursting shells. This continued for more than an hour. Some fragments of shell fell within a few hundred yards of my house.

The pavements are filled with pulverized glass.

Some of the great flour mills have taken fire from the burning government warehouses, and the flames are spreading through the lower part of the city. A great conflagration is apprehended.   **page 468/**

.   .   .   .   .

The grass of Capitol Square is covered with parcels of goods snatched from the raging conflagration, and each parcel guarded by a Federal soldier.

.   .   .   .   .

Four P.M. Thirty-four guns announced the arrival of President Lincoln. He flitted through the mass of human beings in Capitol Square, his carriage drawn by four horses, preceded by out-riders, motioning the people, etc. out of the way, and followed by a   **page 469/**   mounted guard of thirty. The cortege passed rapidly, precisely as I had seen royal parties ride in Europe.   **page 470/**

No. 208 *Evening Whig*, Richmond, Va., April 4, 1865, p. 1.

> *[The* Evening Whig *is the same paper as the* Richmond *Daily Whig except that after the occupation of Richmond by the Federals it was printed under the supervision of the occupying forces.]*

The City

The evacuation of Richmond commenced in earnest Sunday night [April 2], closed at daylight Monday morning with a terrific conflagration, which was kindled by the Confederate authorities wantonly and recklessly applying the torch to Shockoe warehouse and other buildings in which was stored a large quantity of tobacco. The fire spread rapidly and it was some time before the Fire Brigade could be gotten to work. . . .

At sunrise on Monday morning, Richmond presented a spectacle that we hope never to witness again. The last of the Confederate officials had gone; the air was lurid with the smoke and flame of hundreds of houses weltering in a sea of fire.

The streets were crowded with furniture, and every description of wares, dashed down to be trampled in the mud or burned up, where it lay. All the government storehouses were thrown open and what could not be gotten off by the government, was left to the people, who everywhere ahead of the flames, rushed in, and secured immense amounts of bacon, clothing, boots, &c.

. . . . . .

For the distance of half a mile from the north side of Main street to the river, and between 8th and 15th streets, embracing upwards of twenty blocks, presents one waste of smoking ruins, blackened walls and broken chimneys.

After the surrender of the city and its occupation by General Weitzel about 10 o'clock, vigorous efforts were set on foot to stop the progress of the flames. The soldiers reinforced the fire brigade, and labored nobly, and with great success. . . .

The flames gradually died out at various points as material failed for it to feed upon; but in particular localities the work of destruction went on until towards 3 or 4 o'clock, when the mastery of the flames was obtained, and Richmond was saved from utter desolation.

. . . . . .

The fire made sad havoc of the saloons, and none of any account remained. . . . The burning of the saloons is very distressing, as hundreds of people rendered homeless by the fire will be unable to obtain food.

. . . . . .

Drunk with vile liquor, soldiers — said to belong to Garey's [sic] cavalry — roamed from store to store on Main Street, followed by a reckless crowd, drunk as they. With the butts of their muskets they dashed in the plate glass of the store doors, and entering made a wreck of everything with the celerity of magic. Jewelry stores, clothing stores, boot and hat shops, and confectionery stores were objects of special attraction to these pillagers, who, be it remembered, were not Federal soldiers, but Confederate stragglers.

. . . . . .

The order of the city has been excellent since the occupation by the Federal forces. We have not heard a single complaint on the part of citizens against the soldiers, and we are glad to record that the soldiers have found no reason to complain of the conduct of the citizens. We trust this gratifying state of affairs will continue.

. . . . . .

Major General Godfrey Wetzel [sic], commanding the United States forces occupying Richmond, has taken the mansion of Jefferson Davis, corner of 12th and Marshall [sic] Streets, for his residence and headquarters.

Brigadier General G. F. Shepley, Military Governor of Richmond, has his headquarters at the Capitol.

Lieutenant Colonel Manning, Provost Marshal of the Army of the James, is acting Provost Marshal of Richmond, and has his headquarters in the city hall.

No. 209 John B. Jones, *A Rebel War Clerk's Diary*, New York, Old Hickory Bookshop, 1935, vol. II (2 vols.).

April 4, 1865: The troops do not interfere with the citizens here any more than they do in New York — yet. Last night everything was quiet, and perfect order prevails.

.   .   .   .   .

Gen. Lee's family remain in the city. I saw a Federal guard promenading in front of the door, his breakfast being just sent to him from within.

Brig.-Gen. Gorgas's family remain also. They are Northern-born.

.   .   .   .   .

I see many of the civil employees left behind. It was the merest accident (being Sunday) that any were apprised, in time, of the purpose to evacuate the city. It was a shameful *abandonment* on the part of the heads of the departments and bureaus.   **page 470/**

No. 210 Constance Cary Harrison, *Recollections, Grave and Gay*, New York, Charles Scribner's Sons, 1912.

> *[From a letter which Mrs. Harrison wrote to her mother who was not in Richmond at the time of the evacuation.]*

"Dr. Minnigerode has been allowed to continue his daily services and I never knew anything more painful and touching than that of this morning [April 4, 1865] when the Litany was *sobbed out* by the whole congregation.

"A service we went to the same evening at the Old Monumental I never shall forget. When the rector prayed for the 'sick and wounded soldiers and all in distress of mind or body,' there was a brief pause, filled with the sound of weeping all over the church. He then gave out the hymn: 'When gathering clouds around I view.' There was no organ and a voice that started the hymn broke down in tears. Another took it up, and failed likewise. I, then, with a tremendous struggle for self-control, stood up in the corner of the pew and sang alone. At the words, 'Thou Savior see'st the tears I shed,' there was again a great burst of crying and sobbing all over the church. I wanted to break down dreadfully, but I held on and carried the hymn to the end. As we left the church, many people came up and squeezed my hand and tried to speak, but could not. Just then a splendid military band was passing, the like of which we had not heard in years. The great swell of its triumphant music seemed to mock the shabby broken-spirited congregation defiling out of the gray old church buried in shadows, where in early Richmond days a theatre with many well-known citizens was burned. That was one of the tremendous moments of feeling I experienced that week."   **page 215/**

No. 211   Judith W. McGuire, *Diary of a Southern Refugee,* New York, E. J. Hale & Son, 1867.

April 5, 1865: I feel as if we were groping in the dark; no one knows what to do. The Yankees, so far, have behaved humanely. As usual, they begin with confessions of kindness to those whom they have ruined without justifiable cause, without reasonable motive, without right to be here, or anywhere else within the Southern boundary. General Ord is said to be polite and gentlemanly, and seems to do every thing in his power to lessen the horrors of this dire calamity. Other officers are kind in their departments, and the negro regiments look quite subdued. No one can tell how long this will last. Norfolk had its day of grace, and even New Orleans was not down-trodden at once. There are already apprehensions of evil. Is the Church to **page 349/**   pray for a Northern President? How is it possible, except as we pray for all other sinners? But I pause for further developments.   **page 350/**

No. 212   Mrs. Roger A. Pryor, *Reminiscences of Peace and War,* New York, The Macmillan Company, 1905.

[Another letter from Mrs. Pryor's friend "Agnes" in Richmond.]

Richmond, April 5, 1865.

My dear: — I am not at all sure you will ever receive this letter, but I shall risk it. *First* I join you in humble thanks to God for the great mercy accorded both of us. Your General lives. My Colonel lives. What words can express our gratitude? What is the loss of home and goods compared with the loss of our own flesh and blood? Alas! Alas! for those who have lost all!

I am sure you will have heard the grewsome [sic] story of Richmond's evacuation. I was at St. Paul's Sunday, April 1 [sic], when a note was handed to President Davis. He rose instantly, and walked down the aisle — his face set so we could read nothing. . . . As soon as I reached the hotel I wrote a note to the proprietor, asking for news. He answered that grave tidings had come from Petersburg, and for himself he was by no means sure we could hold Richmond. He requested me to keep quiet and not encourage a tendency to excitement or panic. At first I thought I would read my service in the quiet of my little sky parlor at the Spotswood, but I was literally in a fever of anxiety. I descended   **page 354/**   to the parlor. Nobody was there except two or three children with their nurses. Later in the afternoon I walked out and met Mr. James Lyons. He said there was no use in further evading the truth. The lines were broken at Petersburg and that town and Richmond would be surrendered late at night — he was going out himself with the mayor and Judge Meredith with a flag of truce and surrender the city. Trains were already fired to carry the archives and bank officials. The President and his Cabinet would probably leave at the same time.

"And you, Judge?"

"I shall stand my ground. I have a sick family, and we must take our chances together."

"Then, seriously — really and truly — Richmond is to be given up, after all, to the enemy."

"Nothing less! And we are going to have a rough time, I imagine."

I could not be satisfied until I had seen Judge Campbell, upon whom we so much relied for good, calm sense. I found him with his hands full of papers, which he waved deprecatingly as I entered.

"Just a minute, Judge! I am alone at the Spotswood and —"

"Stay there, my dear lady! You will be perfectly safe. I advise all families to remain in their own houses. Keep quiet. I am glad to know the Colonel is safe. He may be with you soon now."

With this advice I return and mightily reassured and comforted the proprietor of the Spotswood. He immediately caused notice to be issued to his guests. I resolved to convey my news to the families I knew best. . . . **page 355/** Mrs. Davis was gone and out of harm's way. The Lees were sacred from intrusion. Four members of that household — the General, 'Rooney,' Custis, and Robert — were all at the post of danger. Late in the afternoon three hundred or more prisoners were marched down the street; the negroes began to stand about, quietly observant but courteous, making no demonstration whatever. The day, you remember, was one of those glorious days we have in April, and millions and millions of stars watched at night, looking down on the watchers below. I expected to sit by my window all night as you always do in a troubled time, but sleep overtook me. I had slept, but not undressed, when a loud explosion shook the house — then another. There were crashing sounds of falling glass from the concussion. I found the sun risen. All was commotion in the streets, and agitation in the hotel. The city goverment had dragged hogsheads of liquor from the shops, knocked in the heads, and poured the spirits into the gutters. They ran with brandy, whiskey, and rum, and men, women, and boys rushed out with buckets, pails, pitchers, and in the lower streets, hats and boots to be filled. Before eight o'clock many public buildings were in flames, and a great conflagration was imminent. The flames swept up Main Street, where the stores were quickly burned, and then roared down the side streets almost to Franklin.

The doors of the government bakeries were thrown open and food was given to all who asked it. Women and children walked in and helped themselves. At ten o'clock the enemy arrived, — ten thousand negro troops, going on and on, cheered by negroes on the streets.

So the morning passed — a morning of horror, of terror! Drunken men shouted and reeled through the **page 356/** streets, a black cloud from the burning city hung like a pall over us, a black sea of faces filled the street below, shells burst continuously in the ashes of the burning armory. About four in the afternoon a salute of thirty-four guns was fired. A company of mounted dragoons advanced up the street, escorting an open carriage drawn by four horses in which sat Mr. Lincoln and a naval officer, followed by an escort of cavalry. They drove straight to Mr. Davis's house, cheered all the way by negroes, and returned the way they came. I had a good look at Mr. Lincoln. He seemed tired and old — and I must say, with due respect to the President of the United States, I thought him the ugliest man I had ever seen. He was fairly elected the first time, I acknowledge, — but was he the last? A good many of the 'free and equal' were not allowed to vote then.

The next day I persuaded one of the lads in the hotel to take a walk with me early in the morning, and I passed General Lee's house. A Yankee guard was pacing to and fro before it — at which I felt an impulse of indignation, — but presently the door opened, the guard took his seat on the steps and proceeded to investigate the contents of a very neatly furnished tray, which Mrs. Lee in the kindness of her heart had sent out to him.

I am obliged to acknowledge that there is really no hope now of our ultimate success. Everybody says so. General Johnson says we may now comfort ourselves by the fact that war may decide a *policy*, but never a *principle*. I imagine our *principle* is all that remains to us of hope and comfort.   **page 357/**

Devotedly,
"Agnes."

No. 213   John B. Jones, *A Rebel War Clerk's Diary*, New York, Old Hickory Bookshop, 1935, vol. II (2 vols.).

April 5, 1865: The cheers that greeted President Lincoln were mostly from the negroes and Federals comprising the great mass of humanity. The white citizens felt annoyed that the city should be held mostly by negro troops. If this measure were not avoidable, it was impolitic if conciliation be the purpose.

.   .   .   .   .   .

Three P.M. I feel that this diary is near its end. [He recorded through the 19th.] **page 471/**

.   .   .   .   .   .

The policy of the conquerors here, I believe, is still undecided and occupies the attention of Mr. Lincoln and his cabinet. **page 472/**

No. 214   *Evening Whig*, Richmond, Va., April 6, 1865, p. 1.

The functions of the Mayor and Police have been superseded for the present, and military law governs the city. In the present unsettled state of affairs this is perhaps proper, and highly necessary. In time we may look for the restoration of our municipal government upon a "Union" foundation, and the resumption of legislation in all its departments.

.   .   .   .   .   .

Yesterday afternoon the Richmond Fire Brigade commenced the very necessary work of pulling down the toppling walls that overhang the avenues of the burnt district ready to descend any moment in an avalanche of brick, granite, and mortar upon the heads of the throngs of citizens and soldiers who are curious seekers among the ruins of once fair and beautiful Richmond. . . .

. . . . . .

Sutlers stores are springing up like pleasant cases all over the business part of the city left unscathed by the fire, and old times are being revived by a sight of the substantials and luxuries enjoyed before the war put them beyond the reach of the citizens of Richmond. People will live, breathe, and move, and have their being once more.

No. 215 Evening Whig, Richmond, Va., April 6, 1865, p. 4.

The transition from enormous prices and a depreciated currency to reasonable rates and real money has come so suddenly upon our citizens that it will be some time before they can properly realize the change. To put the parallel more plainly it is only necessary to place in juxtaposition the prices of certain staple articles before and since the occupation of the city by the forces of the Union. Butter that was scarce at $25 per pound, is now plentiful at 50 and 60 cents per pound; eggs that hid away at $35 per dozen come out readily at the beck of 60 cents, and other commodities in an equal ratio.

No. 216 Evening Whig, Richmond, Va., April 6, 1865, p. 3.

[A copy of the surrender note]

Richmond, Monday, April 3d, 1865.

To the General Commanding the United States Army in front of Richmond.
General: The army of the Confederate Government having abandoned the city of Richmond, I respectfully request that you will take possession of it with an organized force, to preserve order and protect the women and children and property.

Respectfully, &c.,

Joseph Mayo, Mayor

. . . . . .

Good Effect

The ways of Providence are inscrutable. This firing of our goodly city would seem at first glance an unmittigated [sic] evil. But there is another view to be taken of it. It has had one certain good effect. If there lingered in the hearts of any of our people one spark of affection for the Davis dynasty, this ruthless, useless, wanton handing over to the flames their fair city, their homes and altars, has extinguished it forever.

No. 217   *Evening Whig,* Richmond, Va., April 7, 1865, p. 1.

Amusements, like everything else, are looking up. The Theatre Company, indifferent as it is, has been performing to good houses, the chief drawback being candle-light instead of gas-light. But this will be remedied soon.

At the Varieties' Theatre the Minstrel Troupe re-opened last night to a crowded audience. We shall soon have vast improvement in the material of burnt-cork fraternity, and there is room for much of it.

Metropolitan Hall, we understand, is to be opened by a Northern troupe soon.

.   .   .   .

Quiet

For the first time during the war the city may truly be said to be quiet, and life and property safe. Not a noise more uncouth than the sound of military bands and army wagons disturbs the ear of day or night. The garotters and burglars that infested the rebel Capitol either knocked the dust of the city from their feet and followed the Confederate flag, or they have prudence enough to forego the practice of their arts.

No. 218   *Evening Whig,* Richmond, Virginia, April 8, 1865, p. 1.

The Barbers have come back to their senses and old prices again. The following are the established rates now, in Federal currency: Shaving, 15 c.; boot-blacking, 10 c.; shampooing, 50 c.; hair-cutting, 50 c.; dyeing moustache, 50 c.; dyeing head of hair, $4.

The following were the rates in Confederate money: Shaving, $3; boot-blacking, $5; hair-cutting, $5; dyeing moustache, $15; dyeing head of hair, $100.

No. 219   T. C. DeLeon, *Four Years in Rebel Capitals,* Mobile, Alabama, The Gossip Printing Company, 1890.

In the provost-marshal's department at Richmond, shortly after surrender, was the neatest and most irrepressible of youths. Never discourteous and often too sympathetic, he was so overcurious as to be what sailors describe as "In everybody's mess and nobody's watch." One day a quaint, Dickensesque old lady stood hesitant in the office doorway. Short, wrinkled and bent with age, she wore a bombazine gown of antique cut — its whilom black red-rusty from time's dye. But "Aunt Sallie" was a character in Henrico county; and noted withal for the sharpest of tongues and a fierce pair of undimmed eyes, which now shone under the dingy-brown poke bonnet. Toward her sallied the flippant young underling, with the greeting:

"Well, madam, what do *you* wish?"

"What do I wish?" The old lady grew restive and battlehungry.

"Yes'm! That's what I asked," retorted the youth sharply.

"What do I wish?" slowly repeated the still-rebellious dame. "Well, if you *must* know, I wish all you Yankees were in —— hell!"   **page 314/**

No. 220 John B. Jones, *A Rebel War Clerk's Diary*, New York, Old Hickory Bookshop, 1935, vol. II (2 vols.).

April 10, 1865: Ten A.M. It is true! Yesterday Gen. Lee surrendered the "Army of Northern Virginia." . . . There *were* 290 pieces of artillery belonging to this army a few weeks ago. This army was the pride, the hope, the prop of the Confederate cause, and numbered, I believe, on the rolls, 120,000 men. [The muster at the surrender was about 28,000 men.] All is lost! No head can be made by any other general or army — if indeed any other army remains. If Mr. Davis had been present, he would never have consented to it; and I doubt if he will ever forgive Gen. Lee. **page 474/**

No. 221 Sallie A. Brock Putnam, *Richmond During the War*, New York, G. W. Carleton and Company, 1867.

Since the occupation of Richmond by the Federal forces, we have been told by their officers that numerous spies   **page 211/** were in the city during the entire existence of the Confederacy, and were in constant communication with the enemy. They were, said the officers, generally ladies who occupied enviable positions in society, and were in the regular pay of the Federal government. Suspected persons were, however, extremely rare, and we were inclined to believe the statements of those officers admit of much questioning.

A residence there during the entire period of the Confederacy, and a pretty general acquaintance with the state of feeling and society, would warrant us in allowing much latitude to remarks coming from a source which would fain establish the idea that a certain portion of our population, and a much larger portion than there is any reason to believe, were disaffected toward the Confederate government. . . .

The lenity of the government towards suspected persons was one of its most remarkable features, and illustrates the confiding and unsuspecting character of the Southern people. "It is better to trust all than to suspect any of wrong," becomes not a useful maxim when circumstances arise such as have recently convulsed our common country.   **page 212/**

No. 222   Sallie A. Brock Putnam, *Richmond During the War,* New York, G. W. Carleton and Company, 1867.

A tissue of unhappy events had thrown the people of Richmond into the most painful and positive destitution. We have already mentioned the universal circulation of Confederate money. We have mentioned the scarcity of provisions and the usual manner of living. The evacuation of the city found great numbers of the inhabitants totally without food, and entirely destitute of means by which it might be procured. The distress was widespread, and to prevent the horrors of starvation immediate relief was demanded. In a very few days liberal assistance was extended through the Relief Association of the United States and the Christian **page 372/** Commission of the Federal Army, and the United States Sanitary Commission dispensed suitable delicacies, and what, indeed, in many instances, seemed luxuries to the sick and enfeebled.

To give an adequate idea of the extent of the destitution, we notice, from the Richmond *Whig,* that Mr. J. L. Apperson, Secretary of the Relief Committee, reported that from the 8th to the 15th of April, inclusive, 17,367 tickets were issued, calling for 86,555 rations. When the number of inhabitants in the city of Richmond is taken into the account, it will be seen that at least one-third of the entire population remaining in the city were driven to the humiliation of subsisting alone on supplies of food furnished them by the conquerors.   **page 373/**

No. 223   Douglas Freeman, "The Confederate Tradition of Richmond," *Civil War History,* vol. III, no. IV, December, 1957, pp. 369-373.

> *[This relatively unknown essay by Dr. Douglas Freeman was published in 1932 in* The Richmond Magazine. *It was written for a special issue printed as a souvenir of the last great reunion of the Confederate veterans.]*

Richmond was a name in 1860; the War Between the States made her a symbol. She had been the home of a few great men; she became the center of a great tradition. Her ways had been the ways of pleasantness; her fame is that of war. With Leyden and Londonberry [sic] her stout defence won her a place in history; the success of that defence took on the same moral significance that led men to regard the tricolor on the citadel of Verdun as the symbol of allied victory or defeat in 1916. As long as Richmond defied the foe, the Southern Confederacy never lost hope. When Richmond fell, the Southern cause collapsed.

Strategically it probably was a mistake to move the capital of the Confederate States from Montgomery in May, 1861, and to place it within a hundred miles of the frontier. It was done to recognize the value to the Confederacy of the adhesion of Virginia and to rally the border States to secession; but it would have been better if

President Davis, like Frederick the Great, had fixed his capital wherever the course of conflict carried his standard. Had this been done, each of the tidal rivers of the South Atlantic seaboard might in turn have covered the battle-line, as the Tagliamento and the Piave did for Italy after Caporetto, or as the Meuse, the Aisne, and the Marne did for France in 1914. The vigor of the Union offensive might then have been exhausted as the lines of communication were lengthened, and the end might perhaps have been different.

But the decision was made. Congress and the executives moved to Richmond. The Tredegar became the Krupp Works of the Confederacy, and by the spring of 1862, when the first echo of McClellan's guns came in an ominous mutter of hate from the Chickahominy, Richmond already meant so much to the Confederacy that the evacuation of the city, though seriously considered, would have been regarded alike in the North and in the South as the preliminary to ruin. The great battles of 1862 and 1863 made the successful defence of Richmond the great object of Confederate strategy, even to the neglect of Vicksburg and the line of the Tennessee River. The Confederacy was reft in twain because the pride of the administration made it hold Richmond at any price and to construct here the munition works that should have been placed far to the interior. page 369/ Even in the autumn of 1864, when the uncomplaining Lee confessed that Richmond had become a millstone around the neck of the Confederacy, the government was unwilling to face the loss of prestige that would follow the abandonment of the city. When Richmond was at last evacuated, it was too late.

Richmond's greatest Confederate tradition, therefore, is bound up with her long defence against an enemy that was immeasurably superior in man-power and in all the *matériel* of war. No narrative that measures the odds against the South simply by the size of the opposing armies tells half the story. Artillery for field use and for the fortifications had to be captured, imported through an ever-stiffening blockade or manufactured at improvised plants. Virtually all the guns that guarded the rivers of Virginia and Carolina came from the Gosport Navy Yard, which Virginia seized immediately after she seceded. The small-arms machinery that was used at the Richmond arsenal was brought in, in the main, with infinite labor and unregarding haste from Harper's Ferry. There was the direst shortage of powder until the summer of 1862. Harness was almost unprocurable. Hundreds of the horses that hauled the field artillery at Gettysburg were hitched with ragged rope. Not a blanket could be manufactured in the South after the burning of the Crenshaw plant in Richmond. The supply of draught animals was so scant that the army of Northern Virginia was threatened with immobility by the autumn of 1863. Locomotives could not be replaced. When the military railroad from Danville to Greensboro was constructed, many of the rails used on it came from other lines that had to be wrecked to supply them. The South had never produced as much bacon as it consumed, and after eighteen months of fighting was forced to reduce the daily ration in the principal armies to four ounces of bacon, with a pint of meal. A hundred instances of like military disadvantages might be cited. All of them contribute to the picture of a people forced to extemporize every essential element of defence and to rely on valor and generalship to resist the odds against them. Rarely was a major battle fought in Virginia that did not find the Confederates hungry on the field of victory and

unable, through the exhaustion of the horses and the breakdown of the wagons, to pursue the defeated foe. To understand Richmond's place in Confederate tradition, one must try to recreate not only the army in the field, but the engineers busily directing the servants in throwing up the fortifications of the city, and, behind them, thousands of men and women ceaselessly employing the crudest tools to provide the essentials of war, with defeat certain for the army if the machines broke down or the creaking trains ceased running. It is a tradition of hard work not less than of gallant deeds, a tradition of mechanical ingenuity not less than of military strategy.
page 370/

Yet it will never be possible to have these undramatic elements in the Confederate background appraised at their rightful valuation. The eyes of posterity will follow the battle flags. The name of Richmond will conjure up the confused pageant of dusty soldiers hurrying through crowded streets, of white-faced men and women standing on the edge of Shockoe Hill and watching the red flash of the far-off guns at Cold Harbor — a pageant of hurried couriers bringing the news of victory, of ambulance trains rolling slowly down Broad Street or creeping into the station of the Virginia Central at Seventeenth and Broad to unload hundreds of powder-grimed, pale-lipped wounded, still dazed by the roar of battle. Richmond will mean the slow music of the dead march as Jackson's body is borne through the town. It will mean the rumble of caissons on the back streets, gas lights at midnight from the gray house at Twelfth and Clay when the president sat in doubtful council; it will mean the arrival of the "flag of truce" boat when frenzied mothers rushed the lines of returned prisoners in the Capitol Square to see if the sons who were reported "missing" at Gettysburg had by miracle of mercy escaped the death hail at the stone wall on Cemetery Ridge. "Starvation parties" where soldiers danced till morning with cotton-frocked beauties and then went back to barracks with only the memory of a smile; St. Paul's Church full of gray coats and women in black, bowed together as Dr. Minnigerode prayed; weddings with tears; gentlewomen keeping vigil by the beds of unknown dying boys in Richmond's thirty-five hospitals; long rows of upturned red clay at Hollywood, where scores of dead were interred every night with only a penciled shingle to mark the soldier's grave; band music and muffled drums; prayer and profiteering; stalls with second-hand finery that impoverished families had sacrificed; empty markets and high prices; crowded prisons and furtive spies; gnawing want and angry bread riots; threatened raids and the tocsin sounded nervously from the bell tower in the Capitol Square; gambling houses and crowded bar rooms; strutting staff officers and crippled heroes, thronged streets and overflowing homes; anxious refugees and pompous Congressmen; brave hearts fired to desperate adventure; high confidence slowly turned to doubt in the winter of 1864-65; whispers of disaster that passed unchallenged; the hurried packing of archives and the quick departure of trains for Danville; the sullen withdrawal of the garrison; the explosion of the magazines, and the burning of the bridges; and then the funeral pyre of Southern hope lighted in the tobacco warehouses — that will always remain the Confederate tradition of Richmond.

It is not, however, the confused tradition of mass-movement alone. On the contrary, the history of those terrible years gets its color and its romance from personalities. No period of modern history since the Renaissance — not even the

French Revolution or the World War — produced   page 371/   so many extraordinary men in a brief four years. It is Richmond's proud distinction that nearly all these great men, with the single exception of General Forrest, were associated with her in some degree while she was the Confederate capital. The greatest of these personalities was that composite of the 150,000 faces and characters which first and last made the private soldier of the Army of Northern Virginia the unique warrior of all the ages. This is not the place to describe him. It would be too long a tale to tell of his resourcefulness, his unfailing cheer, his sense of humor, his outlook on life, his devotions and his antipathies, his ability to live on scant rations, his endurance on the march, his democratic discipline, his contempt for cowardice, his ferocity in attack, his inflexibility in the face of adversity. Suffice it to say that the highest monument in Richmond — higher even that that of General Lee — rightly stands to commemorate him as he appeared in the service of the South. Next to him, of course, stands his great commander, the simple soul and the magnificent mind that came to typify in eyes of the soldiers the ideal that each man secretly shaped for himself. General Lee's associations with Richmond, though brief, are full and rich. His place in history rises with the years. Although he rarely visited the city, if ever, before the war, and was absent from it for long periods during the course of the struggle, it is not too much to say that whatever is fine and aspiring and unselfish and kindly in the life of Richmond is due to this influence more than to that of any other man who ever lived here. His lieutenants and most of his civil associates were worthy of him. One has only to go to the Valentine Museum and look at the death-mask of Stonewall Jackson to realize that under the austerity of the soldier was the spirit of the ascetic.

President Davis was as true a patriot as either of these, without the glory of great victories to soften the final defeat. Tall, erect, with clean-cut, classic features, cursed with ill-health, half blind, and handicapped by a singularly-sensitive nature, he bore without a quiver the immense burden of the civil administration. Although his very regard for constitutionalism was held up against him as a vice, when it would have been acclaimed a virtue in another man, he must always be credited with sustaining a struggle that would have ended far sooner without him. If he favored the incompetent Northrup, he sustained the brilliant Gorgas; if he kept Bragg in command when that mistake meant disaster at Lookout Mountain, he likewise retained his faith in Lee after the West Virginia campaign of 1861, and found that faith vindicated.

It is customary to speak of Mr. Davis's cabinet and bureau chiefs as mediocrities, but among them were administrators who would have won distinction in any war — men like Quartermaster General A. R. Lawton, General I. M. St. John, of the Mining and Nitre Bureau, the matchless   page 372/   Gorgas, who has already been mentioned, and the indefatigable Seddon who was incomparably a better Secretary of War than Stanton could ever have been. A portrait gallery of contrasting countenances but common patriotism might be brought together of men like Dr. Bledsoe, Judge J. A. Campbell, General Preston, of the Bureau of Conscription, and a score almost as interesting.

The naval group gave color to the capital — Mallory, Maury, Porter, Davidson, Mitchell, Forrest, Sidney Smith Lee, brother of the general, Semmes, after the loss of the *Alabama;* not to mention Tatnall and Buchanan and those whose duty kept them on the coast. No similar company of naval experts ever made greater contributions to war in as brief a time or under conditions as adverse.

As for the cavalrymen, where was their like? "Jeb" Stuart was the ideal of thousands of young troopers — theatrical, delighting in display, with an unconquerable fondness for sweeping raids, yet a moralist at heart and invincibility correct in his conduct. His staff lighted many a Richmond party with their gray uniforms and their yellow facings — Heros von Borcke, the von Steuben of the South, Norman FitzHugh, John Esten Cooke, H. B. McClellan, all of them interesting men. Among the brigade and divisional commanders of the cavalry, was there not Wade Hampton? Did not Fitz Lee and his cousin "Rooney," and "Grumbler" Jones and Rosser and Butler and Robertson and Wickham ride through Richmond streets with rattling sabres?

These are but a few of the personalities that live in Richmond memory seventy years after Joseph E. Johnston marched down from Manassas, and Evans and Lawton came up from the Southern coast for the first great struggle around Richmond. Every name brings up a picture; every career has its inspiration. One finds it difficult to break off when the mention of one leader suggests compeers as valiant and devoted. Surely none can walk the old streets they trod, or read their letters or gaze on their relics in the Confederate Museum and not feel grateful that in that high tradition the humblest son of Richmond can spiritually keep the company of kings.   page 373/

TOPICS AND QUESTIONS

for Short Papers and Library Research

Instructions: TOPICS AND QUESTIONS FOR SHORT PAPERS have been chosen primarily to help you realize that research is a discipline calling for extreme objectivity. (You will read many examples in this book of what happens when the heart overrules the mind.) They are devised as "warm-up" exercises concerned with understanding evidence and evaluating its reliability. Many of these topics will require you to sift and weigh varied information. By the time you undertake your longer paper, you will probably realize that the evidence which you unearth must be related to other evidence within the pattern you establish as the structure of your paper. In writing these short papers, you can use both the source materials in this book and outside sources. Even though you may be writing a paper on a topic suggested for Part III (1863), you may find that information from other parts of the book is relevant. Document your paper according to the method prescribed by your instructor. The number of words in parentheses after each topic is a suggested length only.

Instructions: TOPICS FOR LIBRARY RESEARCH have been chosen arbitrarily in that their primary purpose is to give you practice in discovering and using the resources of your library. Generally the names are of persons who are not well known to the average student of the Civil War but who played important, though perhaps not spectacular, parts in the war. Cite bibliographical references that you can find in your library, the number and types of references to be prescribed by your instructor.

SHORT PAPERS: PART I (1861)

1. Comment on the "high" literary style of the newspaper articles, citing examples. (300 words)
2. In Document 7, Senator Wigfall states that the South by 1861 had no literature. Is he right or wrong? (500-750 words)
3. In Document 7, Wigfall also states that "not one pound of cotton shall ever go from the South to" the cities of the North. Was he justified, as events proved, in making this statement? (500 words)
4. The overconfidence of the Confederate people after the battle of First Manassas was fatal. (300-500 words)
5. Discuss, in terms of the Confederacy, the phrase, "Cotton is King." (300-500 words)
6. Discuss both sides of the Confederate failure to "take Washington" after the battle of First Manassas. (500 words)

LIBRARY RESEARCH TOPICS: PART I

Governor John Letcher
Senator Louis T. Wigfall
Secretary Judah P. Benjamin
Lieut.-General Richard S. Ewell
Hon. James M. Mason

Hon. John Slidell
Secretary James A. Seddon
The Tredegar Iron Works
Fort Sumter
The Richmond *Examiner*

SHORT PAPERS: PART II (1862)

1. Richmond during the Seven Days' Battles (June 26-July 2). (500-1000 words)
2. An appraisal of the Commissary Department under L. B. Northrup. (300 words)
3. It was militarily (right) (wrong) to settle the capital of the Confederacy at Richmond. (500 words)
4. Support with evidence the statement: "In the spring of 1862 the fortunes of the Confederacy were declining." (500 words)
5. How close was Richmond to being evacuated in 1862? (300-500 words)

LIBRARY RESEARCH TOPICS: PART II

General Albert Sidney Johnston
Major-General John C. Breckenridge
Major-General John B. Magruder
Major-General Sterling Price
Brigadier-General Josiah Gorgas

Vice-President Alex. H. Stephens
Brigadier-General John H. Winder
Hollywood Cemetery
The Richmond Light Infantry Blues
The *Pawnee*

SHORT PAPERS: PART III (1863)

1. The Bread Riot in Richmond. (700-1000 words)
2. Economic and material status of the citizens of Richmond in 1863. (500-750 words)
3. To what extent was there "life in the old land yet" in 1863? (500 words)

LIBRARY RESEARCH TOPICS: PART III

Brigadier-General Roger A. Pryor
Rev. Charles Minnigerode, D.D.
Secretary Stephen R. Mallory
Secretary Christopher G. Memminger
Brigadier-General I. M. St. John

Brigadier-General Alex. R. Lawton
Major John Pelham
The *Merrimac*
The Conscription Bureau
The Lee Statue in Richmond

SHORT PAPERS: PART IV (1864)

1. Dahlgren's raid around Richmond. (500 words)
2. The prisoners of war in and around Richmond in 1864. (750-1000 words)
3. Work among the "suffering" in 1864. (500 words)
4. Support the statement that "the old brilliancy and fire were fast ebbing away." (1000 words)
5. Refute the statement that "the old brilliancy and fire were fast ebbing away." (750 words)
6. Religion in Richmond. (500 words)

LIBRARY RESEARCH TOPICS: PART IV

Brigadier-General John H. Morgan
Lieut.-General Wade Hampton
Secretary George A. Trenholm
Major Robert Ould
Brigadier-General John S. Preston

General Braxton Bragg
Governor Joseph E. Brown
Libby Prison
St. Paul's Episcopal Church, Richmond
The *Alabama*

Short Papers: Part V (1865)

1. The people's reaction to the news of the necessity to evacuate. (500 words)
2. In Document 199, Jefferson Davis states that "the sensational stories which have been published about the agitation caused by my leaving the church during service were the creations of fertile imaginations." In view of the accounts of his leaving the church in this book, is he justified in making the statement? (300-500 words)
3. President Lincoln's visit to Richmond on April 4, 1865. (300-500 words)
4. Richmond's "unsavory" element during the war (speculators, gamblers, plug-uglies, etc.). (1000 words)
5. Opposition to the Government in Richmond during the war. (1000 words)

Library Research Topics: Part V

Secretary Leroy P. Walker
Brigadier-General John Pegram
Major-General G. W. C. Lee
Governor Zebulon B. Vance
Commander Matthew F. Maury

General Joseph E. Johnston
Major-General William J. Hardee
The Jefferson Davis Statue in Richmond
The Nitre and Mining Bureau
The "Stonewall Brigade"

Practice in Bibliography

Compile a bibliography of the documents incorporated in this book, arranging them as your instructor specifies.

1775
TOPICS FOR LONG PAPERS

Topics for papers which can be written by utilizing only material in this book:

1. The "refugee" in Richmond during the war.
2. Jefferson Davis as President of the Confederacy.
3. The women of Richmond during the war. (Factual: who were they; what did they do?)
4. The evacuation and occupation of Richmond.
5. The care of the wounded and the sick in Richmond.
6. The people of Richmond during the war. (This would differ from a study of the *women* of Richmond by approaching from a viewpoint of mob psychology.)
7. Richmond in time of war. (Your instructor may want you to divide the period of time arbitrarily —for example, April, 1861, to September, 1863; or September, 1863, to April, 1865 — or otherwise to limit the topic, depending on the length of the paper he requires.)

Topics utilizing some material in this book, but relying essentially on further reading:

1. The part played by V.M.I. Cadets in the war.
2. The treatment of Southern war prisoners in the North.
3. The treatment of Northern war prisoners in the South.
4. The postal system of the Confederacy.
5. The blockade-runners in the Civil War.
6. The logistics of the Army of Northern Virginia.
7. The hospitals of the Confederacy.
8. A study of the newspapers of the South during the war.
9. The Church in Richmond during the war.
10. The general problem of conscription in the Confederate Army.
11. Negro soldiers in the Confederate Army.
12. Richmond during the Reconstruction.